YOU CHOOSE YOUR FAVOURITE PLAYER

For the Football Illustrator GOAT: Dan Leydon
M.O. & S.B.

Remember, our footballers are still playing and scoring goals. All stats are up to 5 November 2025.

First published 2026 by Walker Books Ltd
87 Vauxhall Walk, London SE11 5HJ

2 4 6 8 10 9 7 5 3 1

EU Authorized Representative: HacketFlynn Ltd, 36 Cloch Choirneal, Balrothery, Co. Dublin, K32 C942, Ireland. EU@walkerpublishinggroup.com

This book has been typeset in ITC Giovanni

Printed by CPI Group (UK) Ltd, Croydon CR0 4YY

British Library Cataloguing in Publication Data: a catalogue record for this book is available from the British Library

ISBN 978-1-5295-3099-5

www.walker.co.uk

MIX
Paper | Supporting responsible forestry
FSC® C013604
FSC www.fsc.org

THE FOOTBALL GOAT

WHO IS THE GREATEST OF ALL TIME?

SAKA V. YAMAL

INDEPENDENT & UNOFFICIAL

MATT OLDFIELD

SETH BURKETT

WALKER BOOKS

CONTENTS

HALF-TIME

STATS

CONTRIBUTION

EXTRA TIME

THE FOOTBALL GOAT
AMAL THE FOOTBAL
T SAKA V. YAMAL TH
OTBALL GOAT SAKA
THE FOOTBALL GOA
AMAL THE FOOTBAL
T SAKA V. YAMAL TH
OTBALL GOAT SAKA
THE FOOTBALL GOA
AMAL THE FOOTBAL
T SAKA V. YAMAL TH
OTBALL GOAT SAKA
THE FOOTBALL GOA
AMAL THE FOOTBAL
T SAKA V. YAMAL TH
OTBALL GOAT SAKA
THE FOOTBALL GOA

KICK-OFF

WHAT *IS* A FOOTBALL GOAT?

Matt

Seth

Hi there. Matt and Seth here, two friends who are obsessed with football heroes. We love watching them, reading about them, writing about them and, especially, arguing with each other about who is the GOAT – the player who is the …

GREATEST OF ALL TIME.

Seth
Oh yeah. We could happily do that all day long, couldn't we?

Matt
No, all WEEK long.

Seth
No, all YEAR long.

Matt
No, all LIFE long.

Seth
Come on, mate – don't be silly. Surely we'd need a rest eventually?

Matt
Nah, not me. I can argue about football in my sleep.

Seth
Ahhhh, so that explains why none of your points make any sense!

In our latest football hero head-to-head, we're giving you all the amazing facts, sizzling stats and incredible stories about two of modern football's most exciting young attackers.

Which GOATs are we arguing about? Well, here are some clues: they're both left-footed wingers who play on the right. They've both been lighting up the football world since they made their debuts for their boyhood clubs.

Yes, that's right (or left? – we're confused now) …

IT'S SAKA V. YAMAL!

BUKAYO

SAKA

NAME	Bukayo Saka
DATE OF BIRTH	5 September 2001
BIRTHPLACE	Ealing, London
POSITION	Right-Winger
SHIRT NUMBER (CURRENT)	7
CLUBS	Arsenal
NICKNAMES	Starboy, Little Chilli

LAMINE

YAMAL

NAME	Lamine Yamal
DATE OF BIRTH	13 July 2007
BIRTHPLACE	Esplugues de Llobregat, Barcelona
POSITION	Right-Winger
SHIRT NUMBER (CURRENT)	10
CLUBS	Barcelona
NICKNAMES	Lamine the Dream, Mini Messi

So, come on then… Who is the most magical wing wizard of them all, the new left-footed football GOAT?

Matt
Easy! It's Saka. EVERYONE loves England's Starboy. The End.

Seth
Woah, what?! Look, I love Saka's smile, too, but football's not about being a nice guy; it's about scoring goals and winning trophies. It's got to be Yamal.

Matt
The wonderkid who should still be at school? No way! I'm not saying he's not good, but it's too early to even give him a driving licence, let alone a GOAT tag!

Seth
Hey, if you're good enough, you're old enough.

Matt
Whatever. I just hope he doesn't have a tantrum when he loses this battle…

Don't worry, we're not the only ones who disagree about which of these two is the greatest! There are loads of different football opinions, and this book is all about helping YOU make up your mind. We're going to compare Saka and Yamal – judging them head-to-head on a range of different qualities. Let's take a closer look at the categories:

WHAT MAKES A FOOTBALL GOAT?

THEIR CHARACTER
We'll look at the mental side of the game – personality, mindset and leadership.

THEIR SKILLS
We'll study the full football skill set – physical, technical and tactical skills. And then we'll give you a half-time break.

THEIR STATS
Next up, we'll analyse the numbers – the goals and assists, the individual awards and the team trophies.

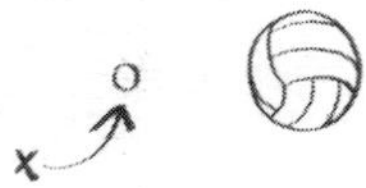

THEIR CONTRIBUTION
We'll end by looking at the bigger picture – how our GOATs have transformed their clubs, their countries and the beautiful game itself!

Sounds like a fair football fight, right? We're almost ready to start arguing! But before the whistle sounds and the battle begins, it's time to learn all about the early lives and careers of our exciting young GOATs...

ORIGIN STORIES: BUKAYO SAKA

Bukayo's path to football greatness began in the parks, playgrounds and garden of his home in Greenford, the area of West London where he grew up. His dad, Yomi Senior, was an Alan Shearer-loving Newcastle fan, and his older brother, Yomi Junior, played for the local Watford youth teams.

So did Bukayo at first, until the age of eight, when his talent was spotted by the biggest clubs in London. Tottenham, Chelsea, Arsenal – he went along for trials at all three academies and was accepted by all of them. But which one would he choose? The answer was … Arsenal!

DID YOU KNOW? The name "Bukayo" was chosen by his grandmother and it means "added joy" in Yoruba. Yoruba is a West African language, spoken in Nigeria, the country where Bukayo's parents were born.

As well as being fast and powerful, and having a lethal left foot, Bukayo soon showed the Arsenal coaches that he was also a hard-working team player who wanted to listen and learn. By the time he reached the Under-11s, Bukayo was on a fast track to the top. So, could he keep following in the footsteps of his Arsenal heroes, Thierry Henry and Alexis Sánchez? That was his dream, and Bukayo was determined to make it come true.

DID YOU KNOW? Current Fulham midfielder Emile Smith Rowe joined Arsenal in the same month as Bukayo (May 2010). They went on to become best friends at the academy.

In September 2018, just days after his 17th birthday, Bukayo waved goodbye to the Arsenal academy and signed his first professional contract at the club. Although he spent most of the 2018–19 season playing for the Under-23s, he did also get to train with the Arsenal first team and make his senior debut. Bukayo was still only 17 when he came off the first-team bench in November 2018 in the Europa League against Vorskla Poltava, and then in the Premier League against Fulham in January 2019. But he showed zero fear, and lots of electric speed and skill.

"He is in the academy, he is growing up and this is the beginning of, I hope, a long career in Arsenal," his manager Unai Emery said afterwards. *Oooh, how exciting* – Bukayo was getting closer and closer to making his boyhood dream come true!

> **DID YOU KNOW?** There's no doubt about Saka's favourite number. He started out wearing the number 87 shirt for Arsenal, before switching to 77, and then to 7!

Ahead of the 2019–20 season, Arsenal signed a winger – Nicolas Pépé – for a club-record fee of £72 million, but even competing with a big-money signing wasn't going to slow Bukayo's rise.

As a youngster, he was inspired by the journey of young English midfielder Jack Wilshere from the Arsenal academy all the way through to the first team. Now Bukayo was determined to become the club's next homegrown hero and he was ready to shine brighter and brighter…

SAKA'S BREAKTHROUGH MOMENT

EINTRACHT FRANKFURT 0 | 3 ARSENAL

9 SEPTEMBER 2019 • DEUTSCHE BANK PARK, FRANKFURT

For Arsenal's first Europa League group game away in Germany, manager Emery picked Saka to play from the start, and the fans couldn't wait to see what the club's top young talent could do across a full 90 minutes. Every time the exciting 18-year-old got the ball on the left wing, it looked like something special was about to happen.

Just before half-time, Saka dribbled forwards and set up his academy teammate Joe Willock to score the first goal. Then, late in the second half, he made it two with a beautiful long-range strike of his own. He wasn't finished yet, though. A few minutes later, Saka rushed in to win the ball back and slipped a great pass through to Pierre-Emerick Aubameyang, who then scored.

After the final whistle, as they walked around the pitch together arm in arm, Aubameyang pointed at Saka, showing him off to the fans. With a great goal and two assists, Arsenal's new Starboy had just arrived. ■

Two weeks later, in only his second Premier League start, Bukayo set up his team's equalizer away at Manchester United. Then England would come calling, and the rest is football history…

SAKA'S CAREER TIMELINE

2019 In December, Saka becomes a regular starter for Arsenal. Due to an injury crisis, he's picked to play at left back, rather than on the wing.

2020 In August, Saka stays on the subs bench as Arsenal win the FA Cup, but a month later, he starts on the right wing as they beat Liverpool in the FA Community Shield. Then in October, he's selected to make his senior England debut against Wales.

2021 Saka wins the Arsenal Player of the Year award following a breakout season, which also earns him a call-up to the England squad for Euro 2020 (delayed by a year because of Covid-19). After a series of excellent displays, including a Player of the Match performance against the Czech Republic, he misses England's crucial fifth penalty in the shootout in the final against Italy.

2022 Saka wins the Arsenal Player of the Year award for the second time, plus the England Men's Player of the Year award for his stand-out displays at the 2022 World Cup.

2023 After grabbing 14 goals and 12 assists for Arsenal during the 2022–23 Premier League season, Saka wins the PFA Young Player of the Year award.

2024 This time, Saka is England's hero as they come back to beat Switzerland on penalties in the quarter-finals of Euro 2024. Unfortunately the Three Lions lose in the final again.

2025 Saka recovers from a serious hamstring injury to lead Arsenal to the Champions League semi-final and, for the third year in a row, to second place in the Premier League.

2026 Saka to play in his second World Cup.

ORIGIN STORIES: LAMINE YAMAL

Lamine's path to football greatness began when he was just six months old in Barcelona, Spain. His parents, Sheila and Mounir, massive fans of their local club, won a competition for their son to appear in a special Barcelona charity calendar. For each month, a Barcelona player was paired with a child from the Catalonia region. Which superstar was little Lamine paired up with?

A 20-year-old Argentinian called … Lionel Messi, who was in the early stages of his incredible career! The superstar meets the wonderkid – it was simply meant to be, wasn't it?

DID YOU KNOW? "Yamal" isn't actually Lamine's surname, but the second of his two first names. His full name is:
Lamine – meaning "trustworthy" in Arabic
Yamal – meaning "beauty" in Arabic
Nasraoui – his dad's surname
Ebana – his mum's surname

When Lamine was three years old, his parents separated. He spent the next few years of his childhood moving between two homes and also two football worlds.

His mum, who was born in the African country of Equatorial Guinea, lived in Granollers, a city in Catalonia, where Lamine, aged four, joined La Torreta, his first proper football club.

His dad, who was born in the African country of Morocco, lived in Mataró, another city in Catalonia, in Rocafonda, the same neighbourhood where the Nasraoui family had lived since arriving in Spain. There, Lamine spent hours and hours playing street football on the local concrete pitches against kids who were often much bigger and older than him.

Thanks to his finely honed skills, Lamine was

scouted by Barcelona at the age of six and joined the club at the age of seven. A few years later, he moved into La Masia, the club's famous academy, where so many Barcelona legends have begun their careers.

As he moved up through the age groups in the academy, the level got higher and his opponents got bigger, but nothing fazed Lamine, who just got better and better. Goal after goal, assist after assist – wow, what an exciting talent he was! As a skilful, left-footed attacker who played for Barcelona, there was only one thing to call him: "Mini Messi"!

DID YOU KNOW? Lamine's trademark goal celebration, using his fingers to make numbers, is a tribute to the neighbourhood that made him. The last three numbers of the postcode for Rocafonda are 304.

For such a young kid, Lamine had incredible composure, as well as phenomenal football flair, and that allowed him to rise to every new challenge the coaches threw at him. By the age of 13, he was already playing for the Under-16s. By the age of 15, he was playing for the Under-19s, and from there, things moved even faster: Barça C, then Barça B, and finally into the first team, all in the space of four months!

DID YOU KNOW? Lamine started out as Barcelona's number 41, then 27, before following in the footsteps of Messi by switching to 19. For the 2025–26 season, he'll be wearing the club's iconic number 10 shirt, just like Leo.

On 29 April 2023, Lamine made his senior Barcelona debut as a late sub against Real Betis, aged 15 years and 290 days, becoming the club's youngest player since 1922! And although he was only on the pitch for ten minutes, he still almost grabbed his first assist with a beautiful pass to Ousmane Dembélé.

There was no doubt that Barcelona's new wonderkid would get plenty more opportunities next season…

YAMAL'S BREAKTHROUGH MOMENT

VILLARREAL 3 | 4 BARCELONA

27 AUGUST 2023
ESTADIO DE LA CERÁMICA, VILLARREAL

As Yamal walked out for only his second-ever start in Spain's top division, La Liga, the Barcelona supporters were wondering what to expect from their young star. But instead of looking nervous and new, Yamal tormented the opposition defenders like he'd been doing it for years. Early in the first half, he cut inside off the right wing and chipped a perfect cross to the back post, where his old academy teammate Gavi headed it home.

Yamal had his first Barcelona assist! But now what about a first goal? Early in the second half, he danced his way into the box and hit a fierce shot that crashed back off the crossbar. Then, 15 minutes later, he dribbled across the box and struck the post instead. So close! This time, however, the ball bounced out to Robert Lewandowski, who tapped in the winning goal.

There was no doubt about who the man of the match was, though: Yamal, Barcelona's new 16-year-old superstar. ■

The game's newest GOAT had officially arrived, and from there, his ultra-rapid rise continued, for club and country. The rest is football history…

YAMAL'S CAREER TIMELINE

2023 In September, Yamal makes his senior international debut for Spain against Georgia and scores. At the age of 16 years and 57 days, he becomes Spain's youngest-ever player and goalscorer. Then, a month later, he scores his first senior goal for Barcelona against Granada.

2024 At Euro 2024 in July, Yamal helps lead Spain to the trophy, while also collecting the Young Player of the Tournament and Goal of the Tournament awards. That goal, a screamer in the semi-final against France, also makes him the youngest scorer in the history of the Euros at 16 years and 362 days old.

2024 In October, Yamal becomes the youngest-ever goalscorer in El Clásico – the fierce clash between Spain's two biggest rivals, Barcelona and Real Madrid – as his team wins 4–0.

2024 Yamal wins the Golden Boy award for the best young player in Europe, and the Kopa Trophy, for the best young player in the world.

2025 Yamal wins a Spanish treble with Barcelona: the La Liga title, the Copa del Rey and the Spanish Super Cup.

2025 On his 100th appearance for Barcelona, Yamal scores a beauty in the Champions League semi-final against Inter Milan.

2025 In the UEFA Nations League final, Yamal scores two goals against France in the semi-final, but Spain then lose to Portugal in the final.

2026 Yamal to play in his first World Cup.

OK, so now that we've got to know our wing wizards a little better, it's time to start comparing the data on these two superstars. But before the battle gets underway, a quick reminder of the three Cs of Football GOAT-ing.

We're going to keep things:

Calm • Clean • Clever

Seth
Hmm, that last one might be a struggle for you.

Matt
Ha, you wish! At school, I was always a star student like Saka.

Seth
Well, I was a young genius like Yamal.

Matt
I bet you had blond highlights and braces, too!

Seth
Wait, how did you know that?! Have you been speaking to my mum again?

Matt
Err, moving swiftly on – let's kick off with Character!

THE FOOTBALL GOAT
SAKA V. YAMAL

CHARACTER

WHAT IS CHARACTER?

Before we get on to what makes Saka and Yamal such incredible footballers, we're going to start by looking at what makes them such incredible people, both on and off the pitch.

It's not enough to have the skills of a superstar. You need the character of a champion, too! Because if you don't have self-confidence and resilience, how are you going to shine when the pressure's on? As Italian football legend Andrea Pirlo once put it, "Football is played with the head. Your feet are just the tools."

So that's why, in the first section, we're starting by looking at Saka and Yamal's characters. We're going to analyse:

PERSONALITY
We'll look at how Saka and Yamal got the best out of their different personalities.

MINDSET
We'll study their mindsets – ways of thinking – and how they overcome challenges and handle high-pressure moments.

LEADERSHIP
We'll end by looking at how they support and inspire the players around them.

PERSONALITY

Saka and Yamal are young, left-footed wingers playing on the right. But in terms of their likes and dislikes, they are actually quite different:

	SAKA	YAMAL
FAVOURITE FOOTBALL BOOTS	New Balance Furon V7+	Adidas F50
FAVOURITE FOOTBALL HEROES	Cristiano Ronaldo and Thierry Henry	Lionel Messi and Neymar Jr
FAVOURITE VIDEO GAME (OTHER THAN FIFA/EA SPORTS FC)	*Call of Duty*	*Fortnite*
FAVOURITE ANIMAL	Dog (he has a cockapoo called "Tucker")	Octopus (he doesn't own one...)
FAVOURITE SWEET TREAT	Twix	Pastry

But that's enough of the fun facts. Now it's time to delve deeper into each player's personality...

BUKAYO SAKA

While the Arsenal fans call him "Starboy", Saka prefers to play things down and call himself "God's Child". Since his big breakthrough in 2021, he has become a role model to millions and a real fan favourite. Here are three reasons why:

HE'S HAPPY

What's the first thing most fans think of when they hear the name "Bukayo Saka"? *That* smile. Yes, whether he's celebrating a goal on the pitch, doing interviews, riding an inflatable unicorn in a swimming pool or cuddling a cute puppy, Saka is always beaming.

> ***"Football is happiness for me."***
>
> BUKAYO SAKA

When things don't go well, Saka never gets too down about it. Instead, he has a positive quote he lives by: "It's not what you see, it's what you believe." And his belief is even stronger than his lethal left foot!

His joyful nature is absolutely infectious, whether you're a fan, a teammate, or one of his coaches. And as well as making other people smile, Saka's happy personality also helps him to play football with freedom, even when he's under pressure, and enjoy every moment on the pitch.

> ***"One of the happiest, smiling and most caring players that you can meet."***
>
> DR GARY O'DRISCOLL, ARSENAL'S FORMER HEAD OF SPORTS MEDICINE

HE'S HUMBLE

> ***"Saka's humility – that for all his talent, he is still keen to learn, to be better – is why so many football fans care deeply for him."***
>
> MUSA OKWONGA, FOOTBALL WRITER

Despite his rapid rise to the top for club and country, Saka has never forgotten where he came from and all the people who have helped him along the way. He is grateful to his parents, who took him to training, and to his coaches, who developed his skills all the way from his early days in the Arsenal academy.

The day after scoring his first senior goal for Arsenal against Eintracht Frankfurt in 2019, Saka returned to the academy with a gift: his signed match-worn shirt, which now hangs proudly on display.

And in 2025, when Saka came back from a serious hamstring injury and scored within six minutes, he raced straight over to the Arsenal bench to hug Sam Wilson, the fitness coach who had been there with him throughout the recovery process.

It's not just everyone at Arsenal who thinks he's a great guy. When asked what made Saka so special, his England teammate Luke Shaw said, "I think he's the most humble guy I've ever met. The most likeable person… Everyone just loves him, don't they?"

Yes, they do!

> ***"The person I admire the most and want to do so well is Bukayo Saka... Anybody who knows him would want him to do well. He's a good human being."***
>
> LEAH WILLIAMSON,
> CAPTAIN OF THE ENGLAND WOMEN'S TEAM

HE'S HARD-WORKING

As well as helping to keep him grounded, Saka's parents, Yomi and Adenike, have also inspired him to work hard in all areas of life. "To know what he was like as a student you just need to know what he's like as a footballer," says Matt Henley, the Head of Education at the Arsenal academy. "He gave absolutely 100 per cent to everything he did."

When Saka was selected to play for England at Euro 2020, the proud PE department at his former school described him as "always ready to learn, so respectful towards staff and peers, wonderful family and top grades". You won't be surprised to hear Saka aced his GCSEs, achieving top grades in every subject!

But just because Saka is now one of the senior leaders for club and country doesn't mean the hard work has stopped. He's determined to keep improving and be the best he can be, inspired by his childhood football hero, Cristiano Ronaldo. "He's always focused, always working and I try to do that as well," Saka says.

LAMINE YAMAL

Both Barcelona manager Hansi Flick and Spain coach Luis de la Fuente have used the word "genius" to describe him as a player, but what is Yamal like as a person?

HE'S CONFIDENT

To make your Barcelona first-team debut aged 15 and then star in the Euros a year later, you have to be pretty confident, right? In terms of skill, Yamal might be more similar to Messi, but in terms of personality, he's more a Cristiano Ronaldo.

"I want to win everything now," Yamal declared, aged just 17. "I want titles and to be the best." When he helped Spain reach the Euro 2024 final by scoring a wondergoal, Yamal celebrated by shouting "Speak now!" – a shot aimed at French midfielder Adrien Rabiot, who had doubted his contribution. And after Barcelona won the 2025 Copa del Rey final against Real Madrid, he claimed that "This season they can't beat us."

For all those reasons and more, critics have been quick to label Yamal as arrogant, but we'll stick with "fearless" for now. Not that Yamal seems too bothered by what other people think, anyway. "While I'm winning, they can't say anything," he said. "When they beat me, they can."

HE'S FUN-LOVING

WHAT THE DOUBTERS SAY

> "Look what happened to Neymar. He had all that potential to be the greatest ever, but not enough focus. Yamal should spend more time practising his football skills!"
>
> **WRONG!**

Yamal certainly likes to enjoy himself. And why not? He's a superstar who's already won five major trophies!

So, whether he's celebrating a goal with his shorts hanging low, making TikTok dance videos with Nico Williams or hanging out with Neymar on holiday, Yamal is living out his childhood dream in his own way.

> ***"Since he was a kid he liked to joke inside the changing rooms; he liked to express himself."***
> GUILLEM BALAGUÉ, FOOTBALL WRITER

"All my personality – cheerful, social – comes from my parents," Lamine once said in an interview. "In Africa, people are more or less like this: loving, close, nice."

HE'S FOCUSED

> ***"Dyeing my hair blond, posting stories on Instagram to respond to critics... It helps me to be focused and has gone well so far."***
> LAMINE YAMAL

When it's time for football, Yamal flicks the serious switch and suddenly there is only one thing on his mind: how to score. Of course, he's blessed with incredible natural talent, but you don't rise through the ranks that rapidly at a big club like Barcelona without also having a fierce will to win and a serious work ethic.

"What I can say about Lamine is that he's very focused," the Spain captain Rodri said during Euro 2024. "The most important thing for me is that he wants to listen and to improve with the people that want to help him."

Yes, Yamal knows he's not the finished player yet, but he's determined to get there as quickly as possible.

WHO'S THE WINNER?

One personality definitely doesn't beat another, so there's only one conclusion here: our football GOATs are *both* winners!

And despite their differences, it's clear that Saka and Yamal do also share some important similarities, including:

- a close relationship with their families
- a love of life, which keeps them smiling and laughing
- a super-strong self-belief, which helps push them forwards to reach the highest highs and lifts them up when they hit the lowest lows

While their personalities are different, when it comes to MINDSET, these two superstars are actually more alike than you might think…

MINDSET

As fellow GOAT Diego Maradona once said, "Football, like life, is filled with ups and downs, and the most important thing is to keep moving forward and never give up."

Although they're both still young, Saka and Yamal have already experienced lots of difficult moments in the game:

- The frustration of finishing second
- The horror of online hate
- The pressure of playing the world's most popular sport at the highest level

That's A LOT to deal with, especially when you're so young, but that's why MINDSET – your way of thinking – is so important. A negative mindset will weigh you down, but a positive, winning mindset can really lift you up.

GOATs like Saka and Yamal don't crack; they attack and bounce back!

Failure! *What failure?* Pressure! *What pressure?*

STRONG LIKE SAKA

WHAT THE DOUBTERS SAY

"Saka's too nice! He's not tough enough to be a superstar."

WRONG!

"He's a bit of a bluffer as he makes opponents think he's too nice, but when he's on the pitch he's a different animal!"

CESC FÀBREGAS, FORMER ARSENAL PLAYER

When it comes to mindset, Saka is one of the strongest guys in the game. With his fierce dedication, fearless attitude and iron self-belief, Saka takes everything in his speedy stride.

- Making his first-team debut aged 17? No problem!
- Making his senior England debut aged 19? No problem!

"Getting knocked down, missing a penalty, dealing with online abuse. He's risen to all these challenges," says Saka's old Arsenal academy manager Per Mertesacker. Speaking of missed penalties, let's look at how Saka bounced back from one of his most heartbreaking moments…

FROM PENALTY ZERO TO PENALTY HERO

Making it through to the Euro 2020 final was a dream come true for Saka and his England teammates. To make it even more perfect, they would be playing Italy at Wembley, in front of a home crowd of 67,000 fans! So, when Luke Shaw opened the scoring after just two minutes, it really seemed like it was meant to be for England.

But no, in the second half, Italy fought back to equalize, and when neither team could find a winning goal before the final whistle, or during extra time, the Euro 2020 final went all the way to a penalty shootout. Based on his players' performances in training, England manager Gareth Southgate felt confident about his top five takers. But now it was time for them to step up to the spot…

- Captain Harry Kane … scored!
- Harry Maguire … scored!

So far, so good, because Italy missed their second spot-kick, but then:

- Marcus Rashford … hit the post!
- Jadon Sancho … had his shot saved!

Uh-oh, was that game over and trophy lost? No, when Italy missed again, England's final taker had the chance to keep his team's hopes alive…

Bukayo Saka!

It was a lot of pressure to put on a 19-year-old playing in only his ninth international match, but Southgate really believed in his fearless young star.

Saka curled the ball towards the bottom corner, but keeper Gigi Donnarumma dived to make another save and win the Euros for Italy.

Saka buried his face in his shirt to hide the tears.

His teammates raced over to comfort him. Unfortunately, however, some England fans were not so supportive. The three players who missed were sent horrible abuse online, including lots of racist comments.

After a few days, Saka was ready to speak up: "I will not let that moment or the negativity I have received this week break me… There is no place for racism or hate of any kind in football or in any area of society… Love always wins."

They were powerful words, but how would Saka's Euros experience affect his form on the pitch going forwards? "He will be fine," said his Arsenal manager Mikel Arteta. "He is such a strong character."

Arteta was right. Two years later, at the 2022 World Cup, Saka was England's joint-top scorer and stand-out player, and then at Euro 2024, he was even more important. In the quarter-final against Switzerland, he saved the day by scoring an excellent equalizer. And when the match went to penalties, Saka got the chance to put things right.

He scored and became an England hero. ■

So what if he'd missed one in the past? He was brave enough to try again, and this time he blasted the ball into the bottom corner. As he celebrated in front of the fans, the smile on Bukayo's face beamed brighter than ever. What a brilliant bounce-back, and he couldn't have done it without his winning mindset.

FEARLESS LIKE LAMINE

Although Yamal hasn't missed any important penalties (yet!), he has suffered other major disappointments, like losing the 2024–25 Champions League semi-final against Inter Milan and the 2025 Nations League final against Portugal.

Were there tears and tantrums? Not really, no – instead, Yamal turns his setbacks into extra motivation for the future. For example, the day after the Inter defeat, he declared, "I will fulfil my promise and bring the Champions League to Barcelona."

What stands out most about Yamal's strong mindset, however, is the way he handles the pressure of being football's "next big thing".

The answer, according to the player himself, is to just ignore it.

> ***"You only feel pressure when you think about it. If you enjoy what you do and have fun, you don't have pressure. That's what I always try."***
>
> LAMINE YAMAL

So, no big-match nerves then? "I left all my fears in the park of my neighbourhood," Yamal says. And what better way to prove it than by starring for Spain on the biggest stage, at the age of just 16...

EURO 2024: FROM WILD CARD TO WONDERKID

Yamal only made his senior Spain debut in September 2023, but as he walked off the pitch after scoring his first goal for his country, he was already looking ahead to the next major international tournament: Euro 2024.

When Luis de la Fuente announced his 26-man squad, it was no great surprise to see Yamal's name there. But when – aged just 16 years and 11 months – he was selected in the starting line-up for Spain's opening match against Croatia, ahead of more experienced stars like Dani Olmo and Ferran Torres, that was more of a shock.

Was he really ready to shine at a major international tournament?

Yes, he was! Yamal celebrated becoming the youngest-ever player in Euros history by setting up Spain's third goal with a beautiful whipped cross to Dani Carvajal. He then bagged two more assists in victories over Georgia in the round of 16 and

Germany in the quarter-final. Soon the only thing missing was a first goal of his own…

As the Spain team travelled to the stadium for the semi-final against France, most of the players were feeling nervous, but Yamal? "He was … asleep!" marvelled his friend and teammate Nico Williams. "How can he fall asleep before such an important match?"

Once the game started, Spain found themselves 1–0 down after only eight minutes. How were they going to turn things around, and who was going to lead the way?

The answer was the youngest player on the pitch. From just outside the box, Yamal curled a stunning shot into the top corner. Wow! What a wondergoal from a wonderkid, four days before his 17th birthday!

Yamal had just become the youngest-ever scorer in Euros history.

After that moment of magic, Spain went on to beat France and set up a Euro 2024 final against Saka's England. How would football's fearless young superstar get on in the biggest game of them all? Early in the second half, Yamal cut through the England defence and delivered a clever pass into the path of Nico Williams… 1–0!

With his fourth assist of the tournament, Yamal had made the difference for his team yet again. The match ended 2–1 to Spain. When the final whistle blew, they were the new Champions of Europe, and Yamal was a trophy winner.

"He doesn't overthink things. He's not afraid – he's not afraid of failing, he's not afraid of disappointing, he thinks of nothing but the ball. And that is often what makes footballers great, isn't it?"

AITANA BONMATÍ,
BARCELONA AND SPAIN MIDFIELDER

WHO'S THE WINNER?

When it comes to dealing with pressure and disappointment, Saka and Yamal have both shown incredible resilience, so we think this one is too close to call! Now there's one final category we need to consider: leadership.

LEADERSHIP

Loud and proud, calm and quiet, fun and friendly – there are lots of different ways to be a leader, but one thing that all football GOATs share is an ability to inspire the teammates around them.

So, what about Saka and Yamal? Although they're both still young, that doesn't mean that they can't be leaders. In fact, because of their super-skills and winning mindsets, their teammates already listen to them and look to them for answers on the pitch.

But do they have what it takes to be future captains of club and country? Let's find out…

SAKA: LEADING BY EXAMPLE

For Saka, leadership is something that is done quietly but with a big impact. "Leadership is doing the right things when no one's watching," he said. "Making the right choices every day."

Now that he's a more experienced player, Saka is taking on extra responsibilities. Ahead of Euro 2024, he was asked to join England's senior leadership group alongside Harry Kane, Kyle Walker, Declan Rice and Jude Bellingham.

When Arsenal captain Martin Ødegaard got injured in September 2024, Saka wore the armband instead. "He's grown into a leader in the team,"Ødegaard said. He's the one helping and encouraging his younger club teammates, especially Myles Lewis-Skelly and Ethan Nwaneri.

So, what kind of captain is he? "I'll speak when I feel I need to speak," Saka admits. "But apart from that, I'm more of a lead-by-example guy."

By working hard and never giving up, Saka inspires his team. And one particular game really showed just what a strong leader he can be…

SAKA SAVES THE DAY!

ARSENAL 3 | 1 SOUTHAMPTON

5 OCTOBER 2024 • EMIRATES STADIUM, LONDON

When the Gunners went 1–0 down early in the second half of an important Premier League match, Saka was determined to turn things around for his team. Just three minutes later, he won the ball back in midfield and quickly slipped a brilliant pass through for Kai Havertz to equalize.

"Come onnnn!" Saka cried out as he grabbed the ball and carried it back to the halfway line. Now Arsenal needed a winner.

Moments later, their captain Jorginho was subbed off, and before he left the pitch, he passed the armband on to … Saka! Wearing his extra responsibility with pride, Arsenal's Starboy pushed forwards on the attack and his teammates followed. With 20 minutes to go, Saka dribbled in off the right wing and delivered a perfect cross to Gabriel Martinelli at the back post. Then, in the final moments, Saka burst into the box to score the third goal himself.

Arsenal's comeback was complete, and it was all thanks to their new leader. ■

YAMAL: CAPTAIN OF THE FUTURE

Yamal is nearly six years younger than Saka, and as yet hasn't been given many leadership responsibilities, but it is definitely part of his long-term plan.

"It would be a dream for me to be Barça captain," Yamal said in March 2024.

He's on the right path already, but hey, what's the rush? The club has five official team leaders – Marc-André ter Stegen, Ronald Araújo, Frenkie de Jong, Raphinha and Pedri – plus experienced striker Robert Lewandowski, who (no offence) is old enough to be Yamal's dad!

In the Spain national team, Yamal has Álvaro Morata, Rodri and Dani Carvajal alongside him, so he doesn't need to take on any extra responsibilities

But while Yamal doesn't often use his voice to speak up, he's never shy to let his skilful feet do the talking. And when his team need a goal, he's already one of the key players they turn to...

YAMAL TO THE RESCUE!

BARCELONA 3 | 3 INTER MILAN

30 APRIL 2025
ESTADI OLÍMPIC LLUÍS COMPANYS, BARCELONA

After just 30 seconds of their Champions League semi-final first leg, Barcelona found themselves 1–0 down. Fast-forward 20 minutes, it was 2–0. Were they heading for an embarrassing home defeat? No, there was no need to panic yet – Barcelona just needed to stay calm and get the ball to their fearless young superstar.

Shrugging off a tackle from Marcus Thuram, Yamal turned and set off on a wonderful, weaving run into the penalty area. Then as five Inter defenders closed in, he somehow curled a shot through the gap and in off the post.

What a goal! When his team needed it most, Yamal had created a moment of pure football magic, and moments later, he nearly did it again, only this time his strike crashed off the crossbar.

With his positive attacking play, Yamal had sparked the Barcelona comeback, and the match finished in a 3–3 draw.

If he hasn't yet proved himself as a leader, he's without a doubt a player that the team relies on in difficult moments. "Barcelona players look at him for solutions," said Spanish football expert Guillem Balagué. "Certainly other players felt – especially when they went 2–0 down against Inter – that Lamine Yamal was the solution."

And now that he's Barcelona's new number 10, he'll be expected to step up and shine even brighter in the biggest moments. ■

WHO'S THE WINNER?

While Yamal definitely looks like a future leader, we're giving this one to Saka because he's already taking on that role brilliantly. Whether he's wearing the captain's armband or not, he always supports his teammates and inspires them with his hard work and will to win.

SO COME ON THEN... WHO IS THE CHARACTER GOAT?

In the Character section, we've looked at what our GOATs are like as people, players and leaders. But before you make your final decision as to who has won this head-to-head, it's time for us to present our best arguments for both sides.

MATT'S CASE FOR SAKA

Who would you rather have on your football team: a happy, humble, hard-working hero or a cocky kid who changes his hairstyle all the time?

Is it even a question? When it comes to character, there's no doubt that Saka is the GOAT.

During his ascent for Arsenal and England, Saka has shown respect for those who have helped him, resilience when things have gone wrong and reliability in the biggest moments. The fans don't call him Starboy for nothing! And that's before we even get on to his smile...

Saka is also a natural leader, who always has time to help the players around him. There's no "I" in "team" or "Bukayo Saka", but guess what... There is in "Lamine Yamal". Members of the Football GOAT jury, I rest my case.

SETH'S CASE FOR YAMAL

Yamal isn't bothered by what others think, and certainly not what Matt thinks. Do you know something else Yamal isn't bothered by? Pressure.

Yes, even in the toughest of times, this Character GOAT has the mindset that makes things happen. He's fearless and he'll never back down, always demanding the ball, using his confidence to take on defenders and score impossible goals.

He may not have the captain's armband yet, but come on, he's still a teenager! Barcelona didn't give Lionel Messi the armband until he was 25, so Yamal has years for his qualities to be appreciated.

Is he as nice as Saka? Nobody is, but I'd rather have a GOAT who'd do *anything* to win. Thanks to his ruthless mindset, Yamal is the clear winner of the Character head-to-head.

Matt
Yamal could ride inflatable unicorns for the rest of his life, and he would still never be as loved as Saka.

Seth
Well, Saka could be the most popular man in the world, but he'll still never lift as many trophies as Yamal.

Matt
I disagree. As a wise man once said, "Love always wins."

Seth
Who was that – William Shakespeare?

Matt
No, Bukayo Saka.

Seth
Mate, I'm worried about you. You're obsessed with him!

THE SCORES ARE IN:

	SAKA	YAMAL
PERSONALITY RATING	9/10	8/10
MINDSET RATING	9/10	9/10
LEADERSHIP RATING	8/10	7/10
TOTAL SCORE	26/30	24/30

So, that's what we think, but we're not the real decision-makers here – *you* are! Who do you think is the Character GOAT – Saka or Yamal – and why?

My Character GOAT is

....

AKA V. YAMAL
SKILLS
AKA V. YAMAL

WHAT ARE SKILLS?

Picture Saka in full flow. What do you see? Most likely he's got the ball on the right wing. He's looking inside the field, ready to beat his opponent before unleashing a left-footed curler into the far corner. Now picture Yamal. Is it exactly the same?

In Character, our tale was one of difference. But when it comes to our GOATs' skills on the pitch, it turns out Saka and Yamal are very, very similar.

But we're not just going to talk about how well they can shoot, dribble and pass (the answer is: incredibly well). Oh no, in this Skills battle we're going to discuss their:

PHYSICAL SKILLS
We're talking speed, strength and power.

TECHNICAL SKILLS
We'll analyse Saka and Yamal's passing, shooting and dribbling.

TACTICAL SKILLS
Finally, we'll look at how our GOATs fit their individual skills into the team around them.

Spoiler alert: these GOATs are both awesome. But one has to be better than the other, right?!

PHYSICAL SKILLS

"Look at the top players. They play 70 matches, playing every three days and making the difference. To be at the top you have to be able to do that."

MIKEL ARTETA, ARSENAL MANAGER

Football has never been more physical. Players are playing more games and those games are more intense. Opponents run faster for longer, are stronger than ever and more powerful. To be counted as one of the best players in the world, our GOATs' physical skills must allow them to …

- Power past opponents
- Jump over tackles and up for headers
- Play at their best level for 90 minutes, without getting tired

Saka and Yamal are both world-beaters. But what makes their skills stand out from the rest?

DID YOU KNOW? Saka and Yamal are roughly the same height (1.8 metres) and the same weight (72 kilograms)!

BUKAYO SAKA

As a kid, Saka had skills that set him apart, but his academy coaches wondered if that was just because he had an early growth spurt. But when Saka began to play against adults, everyone realized that Saka's physical skills were elite!

HE'S SUPER SPEEDY

Don't believe us? Ask Italy's Giorgio Chiellini. In the Euro 2020 final, when Saka went to charge past Chiellini yet again, instead of giving chase, the Italian famously grabbed Saka by the collar and hauled him to the ground. Ouch!

With a recorded top speed of 22.6 miles per hour (36.4 kilometres per hour), Saka simply knocks it past defenders and runs. And he can do it all game: Saka runs up to 7.1 miles (11.5 kilometres) per game, with a whopping 1.9 miles (3 kilometres) of that at high intensity! He's so quick off the mark that former Arsenal manager Unai Emery called him "Correcaminos" – Spanish for "Roadrunner".

HE'S STRONG

Don't let the youthful face fool you: there's no

messing with Saka. Given the rough treatment that he receives, he has no option but to be strong. Saka's style of play means that defenders constantly snap at his heels. But thanks to Saka's upper body strength, clever body positioning and brilliant balance, he can hold them off!

> *"Saka is crazy strong. He's one of the strongest players, pound for pound, I've played against."*
>
> ANTONEE ROBINSON, FULHAM FULL BACK

HE'S FIT

For many modern managers, availability is the best ability. And few players are as available as Saka. Thanks to his clean-living, disciplined training, determined mindset and all-round physical fitness, Saka has already played an enormous number of games:

- 87 consecutive Premier League games by the age of 21 – an Arsenal record for most games in a row.
- 129 Premier League games by the age of 22 – just five players in history managed more by the same age!

When Arsenal play, Saka is there, full of energy and ready to give his all.

LAMINE YAMAL

Footballers don't hit their physical peak until their mid to late twenties. That means that Yamal has YEARS to grow stronger, build his muscles, and become more powerful. Surely that must be a scary thought for defenders, because Yamal's already got some pretty epic physical skills…

HE'S EXPLOSIVE

Being explosive is a cheat code for a winger like Yamal. While his top speed isn't *quite* as quick as Saka's, Yamal is exceptional at rapidly getting up to speed.

TOP SPEED AT EURO 2024

SAKA	20.82 mph (33.5 kmph)
YAMAL	20.69 mph (33.3 kmph)

He's more explosive than a box full of dynamite. Pass him the ball and – BOOM – he'll burst past you. Thanks to his ace acceleration, Yamal can go from 0 to 100 in a matter of footsteps.

> ***"If you have players with the speed of Lamine [Yamal] ... that gives you something else."***
>
> LUIS DE LA FUENTE, SPAIN MANAGER

HE'S AGILE

Route blocked and he can't accelerate? Not a problem. Thanks to his awesome agility, Yamal can reroute in seconds, by twisting and turning past defenders. He may have a slight build, but that allows him to change direction quickly and effortlessly, shifting left and right to shake off opponents before letting fire.

HE'S BALANCED

When Yamal dribbles into the centre of the pitch, he's often surrounded by defenders. While Yamal is no weakling, he doesn't (yet) have the physical strength to dominate. However, he does have another tool … his brilliant balance.

As defenders come into contact with Yamal, they may succeed in touching him, but that doesn't always mean they can stop him. Yamal has such good balance that he can adjust in an instant when he's knocked off course. He uses his low centre of gravity to stay stable on the same route … and keep on moving at the same speed!

WHO'S THE WINNER?

Saka is older, stronger and more physically dominant. While Yamal might just edge an agility race, Saka wins in most other areas. He's not just got better physical skills than Yamal – he's better than most other players, too!

TECHNICAL SKILLS

Our GOATs may be gifted physically, but footballers need more than speed, power and agility to be the best in the world.

> *"You can't always play at 100 miles an hour. Speed and power without control is useless."*
>
> LUIS DE LA FUENTE, SPAIN MANAGER

Saka and Yamal always want control of the ball, because, with the ball at their feet, they can use their technical skills of passing, shooting and scoring to make the difference for their team.

But which one of them has the best technical skills?

BUKAYO SAKA

PASSING

Saka definitely isn't the kind of selfish winger who wants to do everything himself. He loves linking up with his teammates so he can play sharp one-twos, defence-splitting through balls, in-swinging crosses to the back post and ridiculously accurate corners.

> *"He is always looking to combine with other players and make runs."*
>
> PHILIP LAHM, EX-BAYERN MUNICH AND GERMANY PLAYER

Yep, Saka's an (almost) perfect passer – and an elite creator.

Since the 2021–22 season, Saka has created 286 chances in the Premier League, which is more than any other winger in Europe's top five leagues.

And from set-pieces? It's as if he's a robot, always able to put the ball into the exact same area: the danger zone.

DRIBBLING

WHAT THE DOUBTERS SAY

"For a supposedly world-class winger, Saka can't dribble."

WRONG!

Few players in the Premier League attempt to dribble more often than Saka. Across his entire career, Saka's take-on success (that's the number of times he successfully dribbles past an opponent) is 45 per cent – impressive considering that he's often double-marked by opponents.

While that success rate is lower than other GOATs' – including Kylian Mbappé (49.7 per cent), Cristiano Ronaldo (58.9 per cent) and Lionel Messi (64.8 per cent) – Saka doesn't always need to beat a player to cause carnage. He only needs to create half a yard.

So instead of always dribbling *past* defenders, Saka unbalances them with body feints, shoulder drops, hip swivels and stepovers. As the defender rocks left and right, unable to keep up with Saka's epic close control and speedy movements, he waits for the right moment, shifts the ball to the side … then unleashes!

> ***"He has that ability to always get past his opponent. As soon as he receives the ball, if he sees that there's space behind the defender, he goes for it."***
>
> ROBERT PIRES, FORMER ARSENAL WINGER

Through his passes and dribbles, Saka created an average of 6.1 shots per game for his teammates in the 2024–25 Premier League season – and a whopping 1.2 goals per game!

SHOOTING

Defenders aren't known for their shooting, and when Saka burst onto the scene he was known as a defender. But this GOAT was happy to prove people wrong.

"Because I was strong, every time I was in front of goal I used to smash it," Saka said of his breakthrough season in 2019–20. "Freddie [Ljungberg, the assistant Arsenal coach] taught me to be more calm and finesse the ball."

As we already know about Saka, he's a quick learner. While Saka still used his power, he added technique and composure. Soon, his shots became more accurate and varied, giving him more confidence.

PREMIER LEAGUE SEASON	SHOTS PER 90 MINUTES	GOALS PER 90 MINUTES
2019–20	0.67	0.05
2020–21	2.15	0.18
2021–22	2.87	0.33
2022–23	2.43	0.40
2023–24	3.14	0.49
2024–25	3.44	0.31
2025–26	1.98	0.30

Suddenly, he was scoring all kinds of goals: dinks, weak-foot smashes, disguised Mbappé-style near-post finishes, tap-ins and his trademark finish – left-footed curlers into the far corner.

That unpredictability gives him an advantage – goalkeepers just don't know where he's going to put the ball. As one memorable England match showed…

THREE GOALS FOR THE THREE LIONS

ENGLAND 7 | 0 NORTH MACEDONIA

19 JUNE 2023
OLD TRAFFORD, MANCHESTER

With three wins from three games in qualifying, England knew that victory in their next qualification match against North Macedonia would be a big step towards Euro 2024.

But North Macedonia weren't coming to make up the numbers. Saka and his teammates would have to be on top form to get the three points, and everyone would be watching…

Harry Kane opened the scoring for England in the 29th minute, but after that it was Saka's time to shine. In the 38th minute, Saka took on his full back, sent a pass back to Trent Alexander-Arnold … and then continued his run. Suddenly, he was free in the box and when the pass came, he blasted a right-footed shot into the roof of the net!

Then, early in the second half, he scored an even better goal with his left foot. Brilliantly bringing down a long pass from Alexander-Arnold on the edge of the box, Saka took a touch inside two defenders, then sent the ball dipping and swerving into the top corner.

"This is a feeling I can't really put into words. I'm just so happy."

SAKA AFTER THE MATCH

"Bukayo Saka with one to remember – that's on another level!"

roared the commentator.

England's Starboy was on fire – could he now complete his first-ever career hat-trick? Just four minutes later, Saka made a bursting striker's run in between two defenders, and Kane picked him out with a perfect pass. One-on-one with the keeper, Saka kept calm and became an England hat-trick hero. ■

LAMINE YAMAL

PASSING

Want to try and stop this GOAT? Well, he's got a trivela-and-tested technique to trick you. Yamal may be best known for his dribbling, but he's also a tricky passer with an exceptional trivela.

The trivela passing technique uses the outside of the foot (Yamal uses his left foot) to curl passes, crosses and shots around a defender. Yamal may not use his right foot much, but when your left foot is so good, why bother?

> ***"What he does with the ball is unbelievable. Every pass has the right pressure, the right length."***
>
> HANSI FLICK, BARCELONA MANAGER

As well as the trivela, Yamal uses cutbacks, through-balls, reverse passes, dummies and carefully curling crosses that dip and arc towards the back post. With those weapons, he made more assists at Euro 2024 than any other player!

DRIBBLING

Nobody dribbles more than Yamal. In the

2024–25 Champions League, he attempted 109 dribbles – 27 more than second-placed Vinícius Júnior. And in La Liga that same season, he attempted a humongous 9.97 take-ons per match.

> ***"He dribbles past players like it's the PlayStation, and he makes defenders look like cones."***
>
> EMMANUEL PETIT, EX-FRANCE MIDFIELDER

He fools defenders with disguised movements, chops, dragbacks, spins and swerves, two-touch croquetas and the roulette, giving him a dribbling success rate of around 50 per cent.

"He caused us huge problems because we were supposed to double up on him and it wasn't enough," said Inter Milan manager Simone Inzaghi after Yamal had torn his team apart.

SHOOTING

WHAT THE DOUBTERS SAY

"All he can do is score left-footed curlers. He isn't an instinctive finisher, and he's not even that great at shooting."

WRONG!

While it's true that Yamal is best known for his delicious curling, swerving strikes into the far corner, he's also capable of scoring other kinds of goals.

Against Borussia Dortmund in the Champions League quarter-final, Yamal showed his increasingly instinctive finishing with a clever toe poke in a 4–0 victory. Yamal's inventive finishes may not yet be super common, but they soon will be.

> ***"Lamine is going to keep trying new things because his technical skill set allows him to do things others can't think about."***
>
> JORDI FONT, BARCELONA ACADEMY COACH

It's reported that Yamal scored 357 goals in 249 games for Barcelona's youth teams. While he isn't quite scoring at the same rate in the senior team, he's certainly trying. On average, he takes 3.78 shots per match, scoring 0.32 goals per game.

While his scoring rate isn't yet elite (in the 2024–25 season he averaged just 0.05 goals per shot), that's because many of his shots are from a distance and in wide areas – in other words not places that footballers often score from. Yet time and time again, Yamal has bagged important strikes from that exact area...

A SUPERSTAR IS BORN

SPAIN 2 | 1 FRANCE

9 JULY 2024 • ALLIANZ ARENA, MUNICH

It was the Euro 2024 semi-final between Spain and France, and in the pre-match build-up the rivalry between the two teams was heating up. Much of the talk was about Spain's new star, Yamal. But not every French player was impressed.

"If you want to play at a Euro final, you need to do more than he [Yamal] has up until now," said French midfielder Adrien Rabiot before the match.

"Move in silence, only speak when it's time to say checkmate," Yamal responded on Instagram.

The stage was set. Now, it was all about the action…

France wasted no time, going 1–0 up after just nine minutes. So far at Euro 2024, France had conceded just one goal in five matches and even that was a retaken penalty. Spain were now up against it. Who was going to step up in their moment of need?

In the 21st minute, Yamal picked up the ball 35 yards from goal. He looked up … to find Rabiot facing him.

Time for payback! Yamal took a touch inside, then outside, then inside, twisting Rabiot this way and that. The French midfielder couldn't get close. With a gap opening, Yamal spotted a space – the top corner of the goal – and curled an unstoppable strike exactly where he'd been aiming.

"Oh, it's wonderful!" roared the commentator. "Spain's 16-year-old sensation!"

Checkmate.

Yamal was now the youngest goalscorer in Euros history. ■

WHO'S THE WINNER?

In this instance, "GOATS" stands for Great Overall At Technical Skills. While Saka has better finishing, Yamal's dribbling is a super power. Decide how you like your GOAT: amazing at everything (Saka) or a world-leader in one area (Yamal)?

TACTICAL SKILLS

Coaches often play several formations in a game, switching for new situations. To do this, they need clever players who can adapt to different tactics – players who can attack AND defend, who can read the game and who can make the right decisions in the right moments. So how do these two GOATs show off their tactical skills?

BUKAYO SAKA

He's the piece that fits into any puzzle. He can play in attack or defence. The player who's just as happy on the left as he is on the right. Saka's ability to adapt to tactics and positions makes him the first name on the team sheet.

Saka's humble personality means he's always prepared to do what's best for the team. He's already played in every single position for Arsenal except centre half and goalkeeper.

And even after he'd proved himself to be one of the best wingers in England, he still happily played in defence for his country. At Euro 2024, his player-of-the-match performance against Switzerland in a specialist right wing-back position proved the difference. "What a performance," said captain Harry Kane afterwards.

Even when he plays in defence, Saka is a dangerous attacker. "Having Bukayo with his pace, dribbling ability and running with the ball from deep was quite an effective weapon," said Neil Dewsnip, who played Saka at full back for England Under-18s.

That adaptability takes some serious smarts! We've already learned how Saka aced his school exams, but he's also super brainy on the pitch.

"As he got older, he quickly added the football intelligence that you need at the top level."

LIAM BRADY, EX-ARSENAL ACADEMY MANAGER

Saka constantly scans the pitch, keeping track of the changing picture, and then uses that information to make thoughtful, considered decisions – even in the most pressurized of moments.

> ***"Every decision he makes is the right decision."***
>
> KAREN CARNEY,
> FORMER ENGLAND PLAYER AND PUNDIT

LAMINE YAMAL

Yamal may have grown up in Barcelona's famed La Masia academy, but his game was made in the streets of Rocafonda. "When you learn to play football in the street, it gives you more resources," he said. "It makes you more mischievous than someone trained in an academy."

The way that Yamal learned to play makes him unpredictable. On the streets, he had to solve problems in unique ways – such as with his trivela. Now he plays with the world watching, yet it still looks as if he's having fun with his friends.

What's so impressive about Yamal's tactical skills,

however, is the way that he's taken those street skills and adapted them to the 11-a-side game.

> ***"He almost always makes the best decision. That's the hardest thing in football. He's extraordinary."***
>
> XAVI, FORMER BARCELONA MANAGER

It's as if Yamal can tell exactly what is about to happen. He looks at opponents' body positions, assesses their speed, looks at their defensive structure, and uses that information to make a split-second decision. Because Yamal has such a wide range of technical skills, he always has options. Get too close and he'll dribble past you on either side, but step off and he'll play a pinpoint pass, curl a cross or swerve a strike at goal.

Does that remind you of any other Barcelona player? Maybe Lionel Messi?

Though the comparisons between Yamal and Messi are growing with every game, in many ways his tactical skills are more like his GOAT rival, Saka. They like to cut inside but can also go on the outside. And there's also something else that ties them together: their hard work for the team.

In Yamal's debut La Liga season, he made the joint-most tackles of all players in the attacking third of the pitch. When you add those tackles to interceptions made, Yamal ranked in the top 5 per cent of all attackers across Europe's big five leagues.

That sounds like a pretty complete range of tactical skills!

WHO'S THE WINNER?

It turns out the sharp shooters are also sharp thinkers, making split-second decisions to produce match-winning moments. There's not much in it, but Saka's tactical flexibility just about gives him the edge.

SO COME ON THEN... WHO IS THE SKILLS GOAT?

In this Skills section, we've looked at Saka and Yamal's physical, technical and tactical skills. Now it's time to VOTE FOR THE GOAT. We're keeping it alphabetical, and as "S" comes before "Y", Matt is stepping in to speak up for Saka's skills.

MATT'S CASE FOR SAKA

Arsenal's former Head of Sports Medicine Dr Gary O'Driscoll said, "If I could design a perfect Premier League player, Bukayo is very close to it." Well, we can get rid of "Premier League" and "very close" because Saka is the perfect player!

- Pace? *Tick!*
- Power? *Tick!*
- Strength, both physical and mental? *Big Double Tick!*

On the ball, Saka has the full set of skills you need to be an attacking all-rounder: passing, crossing, dribbling AND shooting, leading to equally excellent numbers of goals and assists.

And off the ball? As a humble team player with a fantastic football brain, Saka is brilliant at doing his defensive work, too, whether he's on the right wing or at left back.

So, forget that one-trick pony called Lamine Yamal. Bukayo Saka really is the Starboy who can do it all.

SETH'S CASE FOR YAMAL

Yamal's physical peak is almost a decade away, yet he's still one of the most explosive players in the game. In fact, Yamal's overall peak performances likely won't come for many years … and yet THIS is already the level he's playing at.

When it comes to skills, Yamal is already (one of) the world's best.

- Nobody dribbles more often.
- Nobody dribbles better.
- Few players have a more creative range of passing.

- And that curling finish from outside the area? *Mwah* – it's perfection!

And he's picking up more skills all the time, especially when it comes to shooting.

If you think it's close between these GOATs I've got a question for you: what were Saka's skills like six years ago, when he was Yamal's age? OK … now imagine how sensational Yamal's skills will be in six years' time.

If you're Matt, that's a scary thought.

Matt
I've just had a scary thought: in this book *you're* sharing your opinions on football. Oh, the horror!

Seth
Sorry, I forgot that I have to keep my opinions super simple so you can understand them. Allow me to shorten my argument: Yamal is better than Saka. Done.

Matt
There's nothing more frightening than a lie.

Seth
That's not true. What about your face?

THE SCORES ARE IN:

	SAKA	YAMAL
PHYSICAL SKILLS	9/10	7/10
TECHNICAL SKILLS	8/10	9/10
TACTICAL SKILLS	10/10	9/10
TOTAL SCORE	27/30	25/30

So, those are our ratings, but now the power is in your hands. Who do *you* think is the GOAT when it comes to skills?

My Skills GOAT is

....

HALF-TIME

HALF-TIME

Peep! It's time for a brief break from our frantic football debate. Matt's off to rehydrate, while Seth's shirt is damp with sweat. We take our arguments SERIOUSLY (and we're sure you do, too)!

While we recharge our batteries for the second half, we're going to leave you with some half-time entertainment.

GENERAL KNOWLEDGE

1. Which Barcelona star was Yamal photographed with when he was just six months old?
2. Which chocolate bar does Saka love best?
3. How old was Saka when he made his senior England debut?
4. How old was Yamal when he made his senior Spain debut?
5. In the Euro 2020 final, speedy Saka was famously hauled to the ground by which Italian defender?
6. What is Yamal's favourite outside-of-the-foot passing technique called?

SAKA OR YAMAL? OR BOTH?

1. I made my first-team debut for my club at the age of 17.

☐ Saka ☐ Yamal ☐ Both

2. I scored on my senior debut for my country.

☐ Saka ☐ Yamal ☐ Both

3. I played in the Euro 2024 final.

☐ Saka ☐ Yamal ☐ Both

4. I now wear the number 10 shirt for my club.

☐ Saka ☐ Yamal ☐ Both

5. Right wing is my favourite position, but I've played at left back in the past.

☐ Saka ☐ Yamal ☐ Both

GENERAL KNOWLEDGE ANSWERS
1. Lionel Messi • 2. Twix • 3. 19 • 4. 16 • 5. Giorgio Chiellini • 6. Trivela

SAKA OR YAMAL? OR BOTH? ANSWERS
1. Saka • 2. YAMAL • 3. Both • 4. Yamal • 5. Saka

SAKA'S GREATEST GOALS

SUPERSTAR SAKA ARRIVES

EINTRACHT FRANKFURT 0 | 3 ARSENAL

19 SEPTEMBER 2019 • EUROPA LEAGUE

Floating in from the left wing, Saka screamed for the ball as Arsenal rapidly counter-attacked. Nicolas Pépé played the pass. Saka shifted the ball onto his left foot, then curled a low strike past the keeper for his first-ever Arsenal goal. ■

TEAMWORK MAKES THE DREAM WORK

BOURNEMOUTH 1 | 2 ARSENAL

27 JANUARY 2020 • FA CUP

Saka took the headlines, but this move was all about the team. Arsenal passed, moved and dribbled their way down the pitch in a 22-pass move that involved all ten of their outfield players. The final pass was to Saka, who lashed his strike high into the net from a tight angle. ■

STARBOY SHINES

ARSENAL 3 | 2 MANCHESTER UNITED

22 JANUARY 2023 • PREMIER LEAGUE

Saka faked to cross, then faced Christian Eriksen. Manchester United's Danish midfielder started scrambling as Saka twisted him left and right, then accelerated, earning enough space to fire a finish from 30 yards. It had such power that it was in the net before keeper David de Gea hit the ground! ■

SWISS SURPRISE

ENGLAND 1 | 1 SWITZERLAND

6 JULY 2024 • EURO 2024

With England 1–0 down and on the brink of elimination, Saka came up with the goods. Receiving the ball out wide, he battled with two defenders. No problem! Saka dropped his shoulder, cut inside then shot through a crowd of bodies from the corner of the penalty area and into the net. ■

RED-FACED ROBBO!

ARSENAL 2 | 2 LIVERPOOL

27 OCTOBER 2024 • PREMIER LEAGUE

Ben White spotted Saka's run then played a beautiful ball over the top of the Liverpool defence from inside his own half. Saka raced after it as left back Andy Robertson struggled to get back. Saka took a touch, then nutmegged Robertson before smashing into the net. ■

YAMAL'S GREATEST GOALS

SEMI-FINAL STUNNER

SPAIN 2 | 1 FRANCE

9 JULY 2024 • EURO 2024

Yamal twisted France's Rabiot inside and out in the semi-final, before unleashing an incredible strike into the top corner, becoming the youngest goalscorer in Euros history. ■

WHY SHOOT WHEN YOU CAN PASS?

REAL MADRID 2 | 5 BARCELONA

12 JANUARY 2025 • SPANISH SUPER CUP

Yamal ran onto a through ball, darted inside, dribbled past a defender … then used his calmness and composure to wrong-foot keeper Thibaut Courtois, passing the ball into the near corner. ■

You'll Never Catch Yamal

SPAIN 3 | 3 NETHERLANDS

23 MARCH 2025 • UEFA NATIONS LEAGUE

Yamal timed his run perfectly, cushioning a long pass over the top of the defence with the outside of his left boot. As the defender gained on him, Yamal slammed on the brakes, burst inside, then fired his finish into the far corner, scoring UEFA's Nations League Goal of the Tournament. ■

Breathtaking Brilliance

BARCELONA 3 | 3 INTER MILAN

30 APRIL 2025 • CHAMPIONS LEAGUE

Yamal shrugged off one player, spun, twisted and turned, skipped past another … before – surrounded by five defenders – he placed his shot into the far corner. This magnificent, magical, masterful goal in the quarter-final was voted UEFA's Champions League Goal of the Season. ■

Derby Delight and a League Title to Match

ESPANYOL 0 | 2 BARCELONA

15 MAY 2025 • LA LIGA

Yamal played a pass to Dani Olmo then moved for the return. Once it arrived, he approached the area menacingly and exploded inside past two defenders. With the angle now opened, Yamal let fly… GOAL! His ferocious strike sealed the league title for Barcelona and was voted their Goal of the Season. ■

GOAT HEAD-TO-HEAD

EURO 2024 FINAL

When our GOATs met for the first time, there was A LOT riding on the match. It was Spain v. England, with the European Championship on the line…

THE CHAMPIONSHIP ON THE LINE

SPAIN 2 | 1 ENGLAND

14 JULY 2024 • OLYMPIASTADION, BERLIN

Before Euro 2024 had got underway, Saka's England side had been the favourites to win the tournament. Now they were just one game away from their first men's international trophy since 1966. But standing in their way were Yamal's Spain, who'd already impressively swept aside Italy, Germany and France on their way to the final.

Game on!

The first half was cagey, but just one minute into the

second half, Yamal received the ball on the right wing. He cut inside Marc Guéhi and Luke Shaw, then played a killer pass across the edge of the box, which fellow winger Nico Williams smashed home. Goal!

Soon it was all Spain! Yamal played in Morata for a great chance, then Yamal cut inside Shaw again and forced Pickford into a fantastic save.

England needed something, and it came when Saka picked up the ball on the halfway line in the 72nd minute. He drove forwards into Spain's penalty area, passed inside to Bellingham, who set it back to Cole Palmer … who passed it into Spain's net! Now it was 1–1!

The rest of the match was anyone's game! But in the 86th minute, English hearts were broken when Mikel Oyarzabal slid home to make it 2–1. Yamal jumped for joy, while Saka slumped in disappointment. Spain were European champions for a record fourth time, while England were runners-up once again. ■

"IT IS REALLY THE BEST PRESENT THERE IS. IT'S A DREAM. WHEN WE WERE DRAWING, IT WAS DIFFICULT. THEY PUSHED US HARD … BUT WE ALWAYS COME BACK; WE ALWAYS WIN."

YAMAL

Wow, time flies when you're having GOAT fun. Our half-time pages have already passed and the buzzer is now sounding, so we're limbering up for the second half. We've already covered a lot of distance in the first half, but just like our two GOATs, we're going to keep the intensity up until the very end. So, let's get back into the action!

We've admired Saka and Yamal's characters, we've compared their skills – now it's time to kick off the second half with Stats!

STATS

WHAT ARE FOOTBALL STATS?

Stats (full name: statistics) are facts that are expressed through numbers. Whatever the game you're watching, you can find web pages full of data about each and every player, including:

- Chances created
- Duels won
- Distance covered

The three categories of stat we're going to look at in this section as Saka and Yamal go GOAT-to-GOAT are:

PERFORMANCE STATS
The big two numbers for any attacker: goals and assists.

INDIVIDUAL ACHIEVEMENTS
We'll add up their amazing awards – from Young Player of the Tournament to National Team Player of the Year, and everything in between.

TEAM TROPHIES
We'll analyse the cups and league titles won, for clubs and country.

So, which GOAT will triumph in the battle of the big stats?

PERFORMANCE STATS

SAKA

	GAMES	GOALS	ASSISTS
FOR CLUB	276	75	71
FOR COUNTRY	46	13	9
TOTAL	322	88	80

YAMAL

	GAMES	GOALS	ASSISTS
FOR CLUB	116	30	40
FOR COUNTRY	23	6	12
TOTAL	139	36	52

The GOAT with the most goals and assists is Saka, but that's mainly because:

- He's nearly six years older than Yamal.
- He's played more games than Yamal.

Let's take age out of the picture and compare their goal contributions *per game* instead:

	SAKA	YAMAL
GOALS PER GAME	0.27	0.26
ASSISTS PER GAME	0.25	0.37
GOAL CONTRIBUTIONS PER GAME	0.52	0.63

Hmmm, much more interesting!

- The GOAT with the most goals per game is **SAKA!**
- The GOAT with the most assists per game is **YAMAL!**
- The GOAT with the most overall goal contributions per game is **YAMAL!**

Let's dive deeper into the numbers to see what more they can tell us about our two wing wizards.

BUKAYO SAKA

As we saw in the Skills battle, Saka's crossing and passing have always been incredible. But every season he has worked to improve his goalscoring.

During his first two seasons at Arsenal, the team was packed with awesome attackers: Pierre-Emerick Aubameyang, Alexandre Lacazette, Mesut Özil, Nicolas Pépé, Willian, Gabriel Martinelli, Eddie Nketiah… The list went on. So, as a fearless youngster, Saka found himself playing in lots of different positions, including central midfield and, for a long time, left back. In those deeper roles, Saka was naturally more of a goal-creator than a goalscorer, and this is reflected in his stats:

SEASON	GAMES	GOALS	ASSISTS
2019–20	38	4	12
2020–21	46	7	10

But that all changed during Saka's breakout 2021–22 season, when he established himself as Arsenal's first-choice right-winger. As part of Mikel Arteta's front three (or four if you include Martin Ødegaard), Saka still had lots of defensive and creative work to do, but he was also expected to add lots of goals, as well as assists. So, could Saka up his scoring game? Of course he could, and he's been consistently improving ever since.

SEASON	GAMES	GOALS	ASSISTS	POSITION IN ARSENAL'S TOP-SCORER LIST
2021–22	43	12	7	1st
2022–23	48	15	12	Joint 1st (with Ødegaard and Martinelli)
2023–24	47	20	17	1st
2024–25*	37	12	14	2nd (* Despite missing three months with a serious hamstring injury!)
2025–26	13	5	0	2nd

DID YOU KNOW? Saka's goal contribution record after 210 senior club appearances was actually better than fellow GOAT Cristiano Ronaldo's! Saka had 51 goals and 49 assists. Ronaldo had 50 goals and 43 assists.

LAMINE YAMAL

From the day he made his Barcelona first-team debut, no one has ever doubted Yamal's footballing talent. But what has surprised people is how quickly he's been able to turn his gift into goal contributions. During his second season in the Barcelona first team, Yamal more than doubled his goal total from the previous year, finishing as their fourth top scorer.

SEASON	GAMES	GOALS	ASSISTS
2023–24	50	7	9
2024–25	55	18	25

But for now, as part of an attack that also features lethal finishers like Robert Lewandowski, Raphinha and Ferran Torres, it's still Yamal's creative stats that really stand out.

With his vision and skill, Yamal has shown that he can deliver a dangerous cross or pick out the perfect pass, time and time again. To have 25 assists in a single season would be a proud achievement for any playmaker, but to do it aged 17 for Barcelona, one of the best clubs in the world? It's simply ridiculous!

And Yamal wasn't just setting up late goals in games that Barcelona had already won. No, ten of his 15 La Liga assists resulted in either equalizers or his team taking the lead.

At the age of 18, Yamal is already a big-game player for one of the most successful clubs in the world, but how do his big-game stats compare with Saka's?

BIG CLUB GAMES

SAKA

	GAMES	GOALS	ASSISTS	GOAL CONTRIBUTION PER GAME
CUP FINALS*	2	0	2	1.00
CHAMPIONS LEAGUE KNOCK-OUT GAMES	8	3	0	0.38
ARSENAL V. TOTTENHAM (NORTH LONDON DERBY)	10	3	5	0.80
TOTAL	20	6	7	0.65

* Both in the FA Community Shield – Saka stayed on the bench during Arsenal's 2019 Europa League final defeat and 2020 FA Cup final win.

YAMAL

	GAMES	GOALS	ASSISTS	GOAL CONTRIBUTION PER GAME
CUP FINALS	3	1	2	1.00
CHAMPIONS LEAGUE KNOCK-OUT GAMES	10	3	2	0.50
BARCELONA V. REAL MADRID (EL CLÁSICO)	8	3	2	0.63
TOTAL	21	7	6	0.62

And the winner of this battle is … Yamal! But in comparing a player from Barcelona (11 La Liga titles and eight Copa del Reys in the last 20 years) with a player from Arsenal (zero Premier League titles and four FA Cups in the last 20 years) feels a bit like comparing turtles and tortoises – similar but also VERY different.

So let's now take a closer look at the one club competition in which Saka and Yamal have both played: the Champions League.

CHAMPIONS LEAGUE

	SAKA	YAMAL
GAMES	21	26
GOALS	12	7
ASSISTS	6	7
GOAL CONTRIBUTIONS PER GAME	0.86	0.54

VERY interesting! So far, Saka comes out on top in Europe's elite club competition, but as Yamal's rise has shown, things can change *really* fast in football.

BIG COUNTRY GAMES

SAKA

	GAMES	GOALS	ASSISTS	GOAL CONTRIBUTIONS PER GAME
ALL MATCHES AT MAJOR TOURNAMENTS	15	4	2	0.40
KNOCK-OUT MATCHES	9	2	1	0.33
TOURNAMENT FINALS	2	0	0	0.00

YAMAL

	GAMES	GOALS	ASSISTS	GOAL CONTRIBUTIONS PER GAME
ALL MATCHES AT MAJOR TOURNAMENTS*	11	4	4	0.73
KNOCK-OUT MATCHES	8	4	3	0.88
TOURNAMENT FINALS	2	0	1	0.50

* Stats include the 2025 UEFA Nations League quarter-final, semi-final and final.

When it comes to the international game, Spain's young superstar is definitely winning the big-match battle at the moment, although it's worth mentioning that for England Saka has often played deeper as a wing back rather than a winger, giving him less chance to score.

WHO'S THE WINNER?

Although Saka does have more goals and assists at the moment, we're giving this one to Yamal because his achievements at his age are truly extraordinary. It seems likely that it will only be a matter of time before Barcelona's wonderkid catches up and then takes over.

Performance stats are only one way to decide which football GOAT is the greatest, though; let's move on and look at some more...

INDIVIDUAL ACHIEVEMENTS

Here's a head-to-head look at how many awards each of our GOATs has won so far.

	AWARDS	SAKA	YAMAL
INDIVIDUAL	Golden Boy Award (best youngster of the year playing in Europe)	0	1
	Kopa Trophy (basically the junior Ballon d'Or!)	0	2
	Laureus World Sports Award for Breakthrough of the Year	0	1
CLUB	League Best Young Player of the Year	1	2
	League Top Playmaker (most assists)	0	1
	Champions League Team of the Season	0	1
	Club Player of the Season	2	0
COUNTRY	Euros Young Player of the Tournament	0	1
	Euros Top Assist Provider	0	1
	National Team Player of the Year	2	0
	TOTAL	5	10

Let's start with the headline news:

- The GOAT with the most individual awards, with three, is **YAMAL**, despite him being younger than Saka!

- Neither player has won the Ballon d'Or award – the annual award for the world's best footballer – (yet!) but the GOAT with the highest finish is ... **YAMAL**!

SAKA	YAMAL
21st, in 2024	2nd, in 2025

Let's look at the stories behind these numbers.

BUKAYO SAKA

Saka is certainly no stranger when it comes to shiny trophies!

- Arsenal Player of the Season 2020–21 and 2021–22
- England Men's Player of the Year 2021–22 and 2022–23

Although he hasn't yet won any Premier League Golden Boots or Playmaker awards, Saka has regularly finished near the top of the charts for both goals and assists:

GOLDEN BOOT

SEASON	GAMES	GOALS	GOLDEN BOOT POSITION
2022–23	38	14	10th
2023–24	35	16	9th

PLAYMAKER AWARD

SEASON	GAMES	ASSISTS	PLAYMAKER AWARD POSITION
2022–23	38	12	Joint 3rd
2023–24	35	12	Joint 3rd
2024–25	25	11	Joint 3rd

And while Saka hasn't yet won the Premier League Player of the Season award, that's because it always goes to a superstar from the club that wins the title, and Arsenal keep finishing second!

At the end of his stellar 2022–23 season, though, Saka did make the seven-man shortlist, and he also followed in the famous footsteps of Wayne Rooney, Cristiano Ronaldo and Harry Kane by winning the prestigious PFA (Professional Footballers' Association) Young Player of the Year award.

It still feels like there's so much more to come from Saka. Can he take the next step and one day win the Ballon d'Or? "It's a dream," he says.

LAMINE YAMAL

We hope Yamal has plenty of space at home because so far in his short, sensational career, he's averaging about one sparkly new award per month! In 2024 alone, he won:

- La Liga Goal of the Month in March
- La Liga Under-23 Player of the Season in May
- Young Player of the Tournament, Goal of the Tournament AND top assist provider at Euro 2024 in July
- La Liga Player of the Month in September
- The Kopa Trophy in October
- The Golden Boy in November

Then in 2025 …

Yamal finished top of La Liga's assists chart:

	ASSISTS
LAMINE YAMAL Barcelona	15
RAPHINHA Barcelona	12
VINÍCIUS JÚNIOR Real Madrid	10

He was selected in the Champions League Team of the Season:

He won the Kopa Trophy, again, and although he didn't quite win the main Ballon d'Or award as well, he was still voted as the second-best player in the whole wide world … at the age of just 18!

1. Ousmane Dembélé, Paris Saint-Germain
2. Lamine Yamal, Barcelona
3. Vitinha, Paris Saint-Germain

So, surely it's only a matter of time before he wins football's top individual prize?

> ***"I focus on playing, on winning, and if it's meant to happen, it will. If next year I win the Champions League and the World Cup, then maybe it will come."***
>
> YAMAL

Finally, let's look at one other type of individual achievement that doesn't always come with a shiny trophy: breaking records!

SAKA'S TOP 5 RECORDS

- The youngest player to score 50 Premier League goals for Arsenal
- The player with the most consecutive Premier League appearances for Arsenal (87 games, May 2021–September 2023)
- The first player to reach ten assists in Europe's top five leagues during the 2024–25 season
- The first player to reach ten goals and ten assists during the 2022–23 Premier League season
- The Arsenal player with the most England goals ever

But while those are all amazing achievements, Saka can't possibly compete with Yamal's ridiculous records.

YAMAL'S TOP 5 RECORDS

- The youngest player to win the Euros
- The youngest goalscorer in Euros history
- Spain's youngest-ever goalscorer
- The youngest-ever goalscorer in La Liga
- The most valuable footballer ever!

According to research group CIES Football Observatory's 2025 estimates, Yamal was worth an incredible £340 million. In second place on their list? Erling Haaland at £200 million.

Why? Because Yamal is possibly the most talented teenager to ever play the game.

	GOALS BY AGE 18	GAMES BY AGE 18	INTERNATIONAL DEBUT BY AGE 18?
LAMINE YAMAL	31	129	Yes
KYLIAN MBAPPÉ	7	28	No
CRISTIANO RONALDO	5	19	No
LIONEL MESSI	1	9	No
BUKAYO SAKA	0	0	No

WHO'S THE WINNER?

As much as we admire Saka and all of his achievements, it's gotta be Yamal, hasn't it? As a teenager, he's already won more awards than top players do in their entire careers, and he's only just getting started.

Football, however, is a team game, and winning the top trophies together is what matters most to these GOATs.

TEAM STATS

When it comes to winning the biggest trophies in football, our GOATs are already up and running:

		SAKA	YAMAL
CLUB	CHAMPIONS LEAGUE	0	0
	LEAGUE TITLES	0	2*
	MAIN DOMESTIC CUPS	1**	1
	OTHER DOMESTIC CUPS	2	1
COUNTRY	FIFA WORLD CUPS	0	0
	EUROS	0	1
	TOTAL	3	5

* Yamal only played ten minutes in one match when Barcelona won La Liga in 2022–23.

** Saka played in Arsenal's first four games of the 2019–20 FA Cup, but he was on the bench for the final against Chelsea.

So first, a look at the main headlines:

- The only GOAT who has won a league title (so far) is … **YAMAL!**
- The only GOAT who has won a major international trophy (so far) is … also **YAMAL!**
- And the GOAT who has won the most team trophies overall is … **YAMAL**, again!

Wahey, it's a headline hat-trick for Lamine, but now let's dig down below the surface because the top-level stats don't always tell the full story.

BUKAYO SAKA

WHAT THE DOUBTERS SAY

"Saka can't be a GOAT because his teams never win anything!"

WRONG!

With England, Saka has made it to two Euros finals and lost both times, but as we talked about earlier in the Character section, he's not the kind of guy who ever gives up, so watch this space.

Saka *has* won things with his club team, Arsenal – the 2019–20 FA Cup, the FA Community Shield in 2020 and 2023 – but just not the trophy that they really wanted: the Premier League title. The Gunners have got so close, though, finishing as runners-up for the last three seasons in a row:

2022–23

1. Manchester City (89 points)
2. Arsenal (84 points)

2023–24

1. Manchester City (91 points)
2. Arsenal (89 points)

2024–25

1. Liverpool (84 points)
2. Arsenal (74 points)

The reality is that winning the Premier League title is a SERIOUSLY DIFFICULT thing to do! Not only is it the richest league in the world, but it's also the most competitive. In 2024–25, for example, it was so strong that the teams who finished 15th (Manchester United) and 17th (Tottenham) played each other in the Europa League final!

So, when you think about it that way, finishing second in the Premier League is a massive achievement, especially the year Arsenal fought Pep Guardiola's Manchester City all the way to the final day...

SO CLOSE FOR SAKA

ARSENAL 2 | 1 EVERTON

MANCHESTER CITY 3 | 1 WEST HAM

19 MAY 2024

EMIRATES STADIUM, LONDON / ETIHAD STADIUM, MANCHESTER

With one day to go in the 2023–24 Premier League season, the top two teams were separated by only two points. What a dramatic last day it was set to be! Arsenal were desperate to avoid finishing second behind Manchester City for the second year in a row.

If Manchester City beat West Ham at home, then they would be crowned champions, but if they didn't, and Arsenal beat Everton at home, then Arsenal would win the Premier League title instead, for the first time in 20 years.

How exciting! But as the final day approached, Arsenal received some nightmare news: their Starboy had been ruled out with an injury. Saka had been brilliant all season, grabbing 16 goals and 12 assists, and inspiring his team to win game after game. But now the Gunners would have to win the last one without him.

From 1–0 down, Arsenal battled back to beat Everton, thanks to a last-minute goal from Kai Havertz, but it didn't matter. Because 200 miles away in Manchester, City cruised to their ninth Premier League win in a row, and their record-breaking fourth league title in a row…

Arsenal had lost the league title by just two points! It was a painful ending to an otherwise proud season. "We'll be back," Saka posted on social media a few days later, "and we won't stop until we get there." ■

LAMINE YAMAL

WHAT THE DOUBTERS SAY

"You don't need to be a GOAT to win trophies with top teams like Barcelona and Spain!"

WRONG!

Yes, Yamal plays for one of the biggest clubs and one of the best countries in the football world, and so he has a higher chance of winning trophies. But it's not as if he's sitting back, relaxing on the bench, while his talented teammates do the hard work!

No, at the age of 17, Yamal fought his way into both starting line-ups, and ever since he's been proving that he belongs there.

Let's find out more about that incredible season…

LAMINE LIFTS A TREBLE!

After a trophyless 2023–24, Barcelona went into the new season with a new manager, Hansi Flick, and a new formation, too. But would it win them more silverware?

Instead of a front three, they would now be playing with a front four: Robert Lewandowski, Raphinha and Yamal, plus either Dani Olmo or Ferran Torres.

Yamal started the new La Liga season on fire, with three

goals and five assists in his first six games, and there was no stopping him or his amazing teammates. In January 2025, Barcelona lifted their first trophy of the season, after thrashing Real Madrid 5–2 in the final of the Spanish Super Cup. The win was a real attacking team effort, with Yamal, Raphinha and Lewandowski all on the scoresheet.

One trophy won! What next – the Copa del Rey? Lamine set up Ferran Torres to score the winner against Atlético Madrid in the semi, then the equalizer in the final against … Real Madrid, again! And in extra time, right back Jules Koundé won it for Barcelona.

Now, what about the Champions League? No, despite a goal and two great performances from Yamal, Barcelona unfortunately lost to Inter Milan in the semi-final. Oh well, there was always next year!

Barcelona still had the chance to clinch a La Liga victory, and complete a Spanish treble. Against their local rivals Espanyol, it was Yamal who made the difference yet again. He scored the first goal himself with one of his classic left-foot curlers, and then set up the second for Fermín López. Job done!

"It's a dream come true."

YAMAL, AFTER THE MATCH

"It's a dream come true," Yamal said in a surprisingly calm interview after the match. "Winning La Liga with Barça is incredible, but this is just the beginning of what we want to achieve."

And the party was just beginning, too. Yamal didn't stop dancing in the victory parade through the streets of Barcelona. Yes, whether he's on the football pitch or on the top of a bus, Yamal just can't help standing out. ■

WHO'S THE WINNER?

Saka is definitely a winner, but he can't compete with Yamal the Wonderkid's trophies. No one can! Yamal has already lifted four trophies with Barcelona, plus the Euros with Spain – all by the age of 18. So, just imagine what he might have achieved in the next 10 or 20 years!

SO COME ON THEN... WHO IS THE STATS GOAT?

In this Stats battle, we've looked at Saka and Yamal's goals and assists, and their individual and team achievements. Now it's time to VOTE FOR THE GOAT! First, over to Matt, who's sticking up for the Starboy...

MATT'S CASE FOR SAKA

Hey, I know that the stats aren't exactly on Saka's side here, but before you go giving Yamal the GOAT tag, just hear me out.

While Yamal plays for Barcelona, one of the three big teams who dominate Spanish football, Saka is battling it out in the Premier League, where it's so competitive that the traditional "Big Six" group of teams has now expanded and become the "Big Eight/Nine/Ten". Plus, he's playing for Arsenal, a club that hasn't won the title for over 20 years!

So, a fair fight? I don't think so! All of his achievements should really count double.

There's only one football competition where Saka and Yamal's stats can really be judged on a level playing field, and that's the Champions League, the biggest of them all. And guess who wins that battle... Saka, the real stats winner around here.

SETH'S CASE FOR YAMAL

Matt's right: the stats aren't on Saka's side. I could end my argument now. But just to 100 per cent convince those readers who are mega Arsenal/Saka fans, I'll add something extra.

England had been much more successful than Spain before Euro 2024 ... only for Yamal to help fire them to glory.

And as for Barcelona? Well, in Yamal's breakthrough year they didn't win a trophy. What changed? Yamal grew in confidence!

So the only reason that Yamal's teams are better is because Yamal plays in them! And the stats back that up. His record of goals and assists in big games is frightening. The number of awards he's winning is frightening. But the most frightening thing? He only needs to win a World Cup and Champions League to complete football.

Even the most biased Saka fan has to agree that Yamal is the GOAT when it comes to stats.

Matt
Well, I still don't agree, so what does that make me?

Seth
Do you really want me to answer that? Polite version: you're a complete fool.

Matt
Hey. You can't help who you love when it comes to footballers.

Seth
Or when it comes to your mates either, it turns out...

THE SCORES ARE IN:

	SAKA	YAMAL
PERFORMANCE STATS RATING	8/10	9/10
INDIVIDUAL ACHIEVEMENTS RATING	8/10	8/10
TEAM STATS RATING	7/10	9/10
TOTAL SCORE	23/30	26/30

OUR STATS GOAT IS ...

YAMAL!

So, those are our opinions, whether you wanted to hear them or not. Now it's your turn to have your say! When it comes to the stats, who do you think is the football GOAT – Saka or Yamal?

My Stats GOAT is

....

CONTRIBUTION

WHAT IS CONTRIBUTION?

We're onto our final chapter of debate before decision time – and this one ties all our arguments together. We've learnt about Saka and Yamal's characters, skills and stats, but now it's time to find out how they use all those attributes to bring success to their teams.

We're going to assess their contribution in three categories:

CLUB LEVEL
We'll look at the impact Saka has had on Arsenal, and Yamal has had on Barcelona.

COUNTRY
We'll review their success with their national teams.

THE GAME
And finally, we'll assess how they're changing football itself.

It's Arsenal v. Barcelona. England v. Spain. Saka v. Yamal. It's time to decide our Contribution GOAT.

CLUB LEVEL

Our young GOATs came through the academies at their respective clubs and have stayed there ever since. But which homegrown hero has made the biggest difference to his club?

BUKAYO SAKA

There was a time when Arsenal were *so good* that they were known as the "Invincibles". In 2003–04, they went an entire Premier League season undefeated, winning their 13th league title thanks to legendary players like Thierry Henry and Patrick Vieira.

Was it a case of unlucky 13?

While they couldn't repeat their trick of winning the title, they did at least continue to finish in the Premier League's top four and qualify for the Champions League every season…

Until 2016–17, when the Gunners failed to make the Champions League for the first time in 19 years!

And things got even worse from there…

SEASON	PREMIER LEAGUE POSITION
2016–17	5th
2017–18	6th
2018–19	5th
2019–20	8th
2020–21	8th

The Invincibles were now more like the Invisibles!

But then, in 2018–19, a promising young talent called Bukayo Saka made his debut for Arsenal…

Within 12 months, Saka was a regular starter for Arsenal. He caught fans' eye in September 2019 with two goals and an assist in the 3–0 Europa League victory over Eintracht Frankfurt. He then went on to make many important contributions across his 38 first-team appearances in the 2019–20 season.

Had Arsenal's comeback begun?

NEW LOOK GUNNERS

ARSENAL 3 | 1 CHELSEA

26 DECEMBER 2020
EMIRATES STADIUM, LONDON

By December 2020, the goodwill from Arsenal's FA Cup victory had vanished. They had gone seven games without a win and had just been hammered 4–1 by Manchester City in the League Cup.

Manager Mikel Arteta decided to switch up his starting 11 and turn to his youth talent. Saka returned to the starting line-up and moved to the right-wing position for the first time in the Premier League that season. He was joined in the line-up by fellow academy graduate Emile Smith-Rowe and teenager Gabriel Martinelli.

They gelled immediately and Saka was the star of the show! He won the foul for Granit Xhaka's goal then added a goal of his own in a player-of-the-match performance.

"I said Arsenal could go down, and they might have been relegated if Mikel Arteta had continued to play the same team," said former England captain and BBC pundit Alan Shearer after the match.

> *"The youngsters brought energy to the team."*
> ALAN SHEARER

And they kept on bringing the energy, helping Arsenal rise from 15th to 8th position.

But who had contributed the most to that rise? Well, at the end of the season Arsenal's Player of the Year was named as … Bukayo Saka! ■

ARSENAL ON THE UP

As Saka's influence grew in the club, Arsenal continued to climb the league:

- In 2021–22 they finished 5th
- In 2022–23 they finished 2nd – finally, they were back in the Champions League!
- In 2023–24 they finished 2nd again
- In 2024–25 they finished 2nd AGAIN!

Arsenal were back! And much of that was thanks to Saka. In that time:

- He'd been named as Arsenal's Player of the Year in back-to-back seasons – the first male player since Thierry Henry.
- He'd become the third-youngest player to make 250 appearances for Arsenal.
- He'd set a club record for most consecutive Premier League appearances.
- He'd finished as the team's top scorer for three seasons in a row (it would have been four if he hadn't suffered a lengthy injury in 2024–25).
- He'd become a role model for Arsenal's academy youngsters.

Wow, Saka had truly become Arsenal's Starboy, turning them from "Invisibles" to contenders. Next step: Invincibles?

> ***"He is the biggest symbol of this regeneration at Arsenal."***
> AMY LAWRENCE, JOURNALIST

LAMINE YAMAL

Lionel Messi. Xavi. Iniesta. The Barcelona side of the 2010s wasn't just the best in the world – it was possibly the best in history. But by 2021, things had changed. The club was struggling. So much so they had to let main man Messi leave! There wasn't enough money to pay him.

On the pitch, things weren't much better. Barcelona were thrashed 8–2 by Bayern Munich in the 2019–20 Champions League quarter-final, then without Messi they were eliminated in the group stage in both 2021–22 and 2022–23. What a disaster!

When Ousmane Dembélé was sold to Paris Saint Germain in August 2023 for €50 million, Barcelona couldn't afford to buy a replacement winger. What could manager Xavi do?

LA MASIA MASTERCLASS

Well, back when Barcelona were at their best, much of the team came from their famous La Masia academy. So Xavi decided to look there once more. Perhaps that young kid who was turning heads – Yamal – could he be given a chance in Dembélé's position?

Yamal didn't just take that chance. He became a symbol for the new wave of talent from La Masia that also includes Gavi and Pau Cubarsí. His breakthrough came at the perfect time, taking the pressure off the club's finances, helping them to a Spanish treble, and even pushing them as far as the Champions League semi-final.

> ***"We won't stop until we put this club where it belongs – at the top!"***
>
> YAMAL

WHAT THE DOUBTERS SAY

"Nine league goals in 2024–25?! Those aren't GOAT numbers – he can't be that important to Barcelona!"

WRONG!

The main aim in football isn't scoring lots of goals yourself – it's winning matches as a team, and with Yamal on the pitch, Barcelona certainly do that. Just look at their 2024–25 record in La Liga with and without Yamal.

	WITH YAMAL STARTING	YAMAL SUBBED ON IN THE SECOND HALF	WITHOUT YAMAL
GAMES	31	4	3
WINS	26	2	0
DRAWS	3	0	1
DEFEATS	2	2	2
POINTS PER GAME	2.6	1.5	0.33

The more Yamal, the better the result. Yes, one player really can make that much difference – especially in the BIGGEST of games…

MOVE OVER MADRID, BARÇA ARE BACK!

El Clásico is the one of the fiercest rivalries in world football, watched by around 650 million people across 182 countries. But in the 14 matches between 2020 and the end of the 2023–24 season, Real Madrid had won ten and lost just four. What was worse for Barcelona, Real Madrid ended 2024 as La Liga, Champions League AND Spanish Super Cup champions. Barcelona's bitter rivals were dominating!

Yamal was determined to put the power back in Barça's hands, starting with the first Clásico of the 2024–25 season…

REAL MADRID 0-4 BARCELONA

26 October 2024, La Liga

All eyes were on Kylian Mbappé for his first Clásico for Real Madrid, yet Barcelona stole the show. Yamal became the youngest-ever scorer in a Clásico when he added the third goal with his "weaker" right foot.

REAL MADRID 2-5 BARCELONA

12 January 2025, Spanish Super Cup

Real Madrid might have scored the first goal, but after that it was

all Barcelona – thanks to Yamal! His equalizer sparked Barcelona into life and they scored five goals in just 26 minutes to go 5–1 up!

BARCELONA 3–2 REAL MADRID

26 April 2025, Copa del Rey final

Yamal grabbed two great assists in normal time, before Jules Koundé popped up with the winner in extra time. Real Madrid weren't happy – three of their players were sent off in the final seconds!

BARCELONA 4–3 REAL MADRID

11 May 2025, La Liga

Despite a Kylian Mbappé hat-trick, the most brilliant individual moment belonged to Yamal, who was also named Player of the Match. In the 32nd minute, he curled an outrageous strike into the bottom corner.

Barcelona were back on top! They'd played four and won four, finishing above Real Madrid in all league and cup competitions. With three goals and two assists in the clashes, Yamal had become the Clásico King. ■

WHO'S THE WINNER?

Oooh, this battle is even tighter than the areas Yamal dribbles through and even closer than Saka's control. A Premier League title might have given Saka the edge, while Champions League triumph might have won it for Yamal. Don't rule out either eventuality...

COUNTRY

BUKAYO SAKA

"He epitomizes what we're about: he's got talent, he's humble, he works for the team, he's really popular and the quality of his play is top level."

GARETH SOUTHGATE, FORMER ENGLAND MANAGER

England are enjoying one of the most exciting eras in their history. They've reached back-to-back Euros finals for the first time ever and have a squad packed full of attacking talent. Yet one name stands out among all others: Bukayo Saka.

Yes, Saka's name is one of the first on the England team sheet. He's England's reliable performer who can play in any position. His hard-working nature and tactical flexibility give managers plenty of options – whether he plays at wing back or further forwards.

> ***"He is a key player for us."***
>
> THOMAS TUCHEL, ENGLAND MANAGER

EUROS DRAMA

Less than a year after making his senior debut, Saka was *already* an important player in England's Euro 2020 run to the final. But unfortunately, after his bright start, the tournament ended with his missed penalty in the shootout.

WHAT THE DOUBTERS SAY

"Saka let his country down!"

WRONG!

The truth is that England's new era almost perfectly overlaps with Saka's debut – and that's no coincidence.

After his Euro 2020 disappointment, Saka put on a show at the 2022 World Cup, registering four goal contributions in four games and being named as England's Player of the Year for

2021–22. Always the big-game player, he won the penalty for England's only goal and was voted as BBC Sport's Player of the Match in England's quarter-final against title holders France.

The following season, he was again named as England's Player of the Year!

And at Euro 2024, his match-winning performance against Switzerland in the quarter-final ensured England made it all the way to the final against Spain, where Saka also played a key part in Palmer's equalizer.

Since Saka's debut, he's registered 22 goal contributions (13 goals, 9 assists) in just 46 England games. In that time, only Harry Kane has scored more goals for England!

Let his country down? *Pah,* he's one of his country's most important players!

"He's arguably the most important England player because he does something different. He beats players."

RIO FERDINAND, EX-ENGLAND DEFENDER

LAMINE YAMAL

Let's rewind to the last decade: the 2010s. Spain have got the ball and they're going tiki. Taka. Tiki. Taka. Tiki. Taka. Pass, pass, pass, pass, pass … *argh*!!! It was just getting so BORING!

Though they won the Euros, the World Cup, then the Euros AGAIN between 2008 and 2012, Spain's passing powers soon declined…

In 2014, they were eliminated at the group stage of the World Cup, then they failed to win a single knockout match in their 2016, 2018 and 2022 tournaments. (At Euro 2020, they made the semi-final without winning a knockout game in regular time.)

Spain had heaps of midfielders who could tiki and taka. But nobody who could threaten. In their unsuccessful 2022 World Cup knockout game against Morocco, Spain had 77 per cent possession … but managed just one shot on target!

They needed someone cutting-edge.

TIKI-TAKA-BOOM!

Step forwards Lamine Yamal and Nico Williams: two dynamic wingers nicknamed by newspaper *Marca* as Spain's "two Ferraris".

Yamal and Williams stayed wide, dribbled and created. They didn't spend their time passing sideways! In a friendly against Brazil, Yamal set up three goals and received a standing ovation from the crowd.

Spain were changing the way they played. Yamal was at the centre of everything they did.

At Euro 2024, Yamal assisted more goals (four) than any other player and scored three himself, becoming the youngest goalscorer at a European Championships or World Cup (younger, even, than a certain player called Pelé...). With five goal contributions, he was directly involved in a third of Spain's 15 goals. Along the way, he'd attempted 50 dribbles and completed 29 of them – more than anyone except France's Ousmane Dembélé . Such directness was a long way from Spain's tiki-taka days...

DID YOU KNOW? Yamal was so young at Euro 2024 that he had to take his schoolwork in his suitcase so he could study for his exams. He passed all of them – his best grade was in maths.

Thanks to UEFA's Young Player of the Tournament, Yamal, and his partner Williams, Spain became champions again, beating England 2–1! They won all seven of their games and set a record for most goals scored at a Euros (15). Goodbye, tiki-taka. Hello, pace and precision!

A NEW ERA

Spain's run continued into the 2025 Nations League as Spain roared to the final – only to agonizingly lose out to Portugal on penalties.

Still, after a decade of tiki-taka tragedy, Spain's new dynamic style with Yamal at its core had paid off. Suddenly, Spain were the best (and most entertaining) team in Europe – and possibly the world.

> ***"He is a miracle. We're just waiting for him to walk on water."***
>
> JOAN JOSEP PALLÀS, SPANISH FOOTBALL JOURNALIST

WHO'S THE WINNER?

Sorry, Saka fans, football comes down to fine margins and this margin is very fine. If England had won Euro 2024, we'd give this to Saka. He's helped to transform his national team along with GOATs like Jude Bellingham and Harry Kane. But Yamal's Euro 2024 trophy ultimately makes him the winner in this battle.

THE GAME

GOATs don't just score goals and win matches. They change the game of football itself, whether that's through creative skills, never-before-seen tricks, or brilliant behaviour. Though Saka and Yamal are still young, they've already begun to make a difference.

BUKAYO SAKA

"He's just that perfect boy who you wish will be either your son or your brother – who's just been brought up the right way."

AARON RAMSDALE
EX-ENGLAND AND ARSENAL TEAMMATE

Ask fans of any Premier League club who their favourite player from a rival is, they'll likely have the same answer: Saka. Even Tottenham fans like him (when he isn't scoring past them).

Saka's kindness makes him a fan favourite. So does his courage. After he missed a penalty in the Euro 2020 final, he received ugly racist abuse on social media. Saka called out the racism, urged social media companies to stop hatred, and encouraged fans to come together. Just weeks later, Tottenham fans gave him a standing ovation in a pre-season friendly. "The fact that Tottenham's fans are willing to do that for me shows that some things are bigger than football," Saka said.

Bringing Tottenham and Arsenal fans together? That's the kind of achievement that should put Saka amongst the Nobel Peace Prize contenders. First: peace in North London. Next: world peace.

Don't put that past Saka. This GOAT is changing football with his likeable personality – why can't he change the world, too?

LAMINE YAMAL

At Euro 2024, almost ten per cent of players were born or had heritage from outside the countries they played for. However, the Spanish football team has not always been very diverse.

Now that's changing thanks to two players in particular: Lamine Yamal (born in Spain to parents from Morocco and Equatorial Guinea) and Nico Williams (born in Spain to parents from Ghana).

"In Spain there are a lot of people who continue to think that all white people are Spaniards and those who aren't are foreigners," said anti-racism campaigner Moha Gerehou. "In this case we have two young Black men who were born in Spain and who are the leaders of the national team."

Yamal, alongside Williams, shows a diverse, modern Spain made up of people from all kinds of backgrounds.

Yamal is proud of his roots. The flags of his parents' countries are etched onto his boots and his 304 goal celebration pays tribute to the diverse Rocafonda neighbourhood he grew up in.

> ***"It's very important ... we remind people who say that Spain isn't big enough for everyone, or that there's a problem with immigration and that immigration brings crime, of Nico Williams and Lamine Yamal."***
>
> **IRENE MONTERO, SPANISH MEMBER OF THE EUROPEAN PARLIAMENT**

One last (fun) point. Before we decide on our Contribution GOAT, we need to talk about one contribution to the game where they are joint winners: how fun they're making football!

Saka and Yamal play with smiles on their faces and joy in their feet. Such enjoyment has rarely been seen since the days of Brazil icon Ronaldinho. Saka's smile is infectious, while Yamal plays as if he's having a kickabout with his friends in the park. As fans, we love to see players who enjoy themselves – especially when they bring a smile to our faces with their skills and thrills.

We're lucky to have these two legends performing on the biggest of stages. But whose overall contribution has been the biggest?

WHO'S THE WINNER?

Our GOATs play with smiles on their faces and are role models to millions. They're changing attitudes and painting pictures of positivity. We're giving them both the W on this one.

SO COME ON THEN... WHO IS THE CONTRIBUTION GOAT?

In this Contribution section, we've looked at the impact Saka and Yamal have had on club, country and the game of football itself. Now it's time to put those arguments into action and VOTE FOR THE GOAT!

MATT'S CASE FOR SAKA

Arsenal and England – two football teams who were on a downward slide until along came a Starboy to save the day.

Since Saka arrived on the scene, Arsenal have shot up the Premier League table to finish second for three years in a row, and England have reached two Euro finals in a row. I'm sorry, but that can't be a coincidence!

Really, Saka's impact on his club and country shouldn't be measured in results or trophies, though; it should be measured in smiles, joy and magical moments. Because through his happy, humble work both on and off the pitch, Saka inspires people and brings them together – no matter what team they support – in a way that no other player can.

So in terms of his contribution to the game and the world around it, brilliant, beaming Bukayo is my undisputed Football GOAT and I dare anyone to disagree!

SETH'S CASE FOR YAMAL

What happened to backwards Barcelona and sideways Spain? Yamal! Yes, this GOAT has taken his club and country by storm, evolving his teams from their tiki-taka troubles to winning home trophies.

And he's done that ALREADY, in just a few seasons as a teenager. He's bringing football into a new era in Spain. He's already a European champion with Spain, and it's surely only a matter of time before he wins major European honours with Barcelona. Will he become a world champion too? Don't rule it out – he's not just got years to complete football – he's got decades!

Sure, Saka has helped change Arsenal's outlook, but what have they won? What have Saka's England won? Three second-placed finishes in the Premier League and two runners-up trophies at the Euros? Well, guess what, Saka fans… Bukayo is coming second in this match-up too; Yamal is undeniably the Contribution GOAT.

Matt
If we're going to start saying talented teenagers are GOATs, then we might as well write a book on Freddy Adu or Bojan Krkić.

Seth
Hey, they're both great, but Yamal operates in a different league.

Matt
It's called La Liga. Lots of players play in La Liga.

Seth
But nobody stands out like Yamal does.

Matt
Would Barcelona have won La Liga without Raphinha? Would Spain have won the Euros without Nico Williams?

Seth
Would Arsenal have won…? *Oh*, wait!

Matt
I won't need to wait long, my friend. Saka's time is coming. And when it arrives, I'll accept your apology.

Seth
You can have my apology already. I apologize that Yamal is better than Saka.

THE SCORES ARE IN:

	SAKA	YAMAL
CLUB CONTRIBUTION	9/10	9/10
COUNTRY CONTRIBUTION	7/10	9/10
GAME CONTRIBUTION	8/10	8/10
TOTAL SCORE	24/30	26/30

Those are our opinions, but do you agree? Who do you think is the Contribution GOAT – Saka or Yamal?

My Contribution GOAT is

....

EXTRA TIME
THE FOOTBALL
AKA V. YAMAL

That's it for the main action, but is there anything to separate our two challengers? Despite all our discussion, we're still in disagreement. So, we're heading into extra time…

CHARACTER

	Saka	Yamal
CHARACTER	He's happy, humble and hard-working!	He's confident, fun-loving and focused!
	Resilience? He's got it by the bucket-load.	Pressure? This fearless teen doesn't know what that means.
	He leads on AND off the pitch for club and country.	He may not wear the armband, but he's always willing to take responsibility.

SKILLS

	Saka	Yamal
SKILLS	Beep, beep! "Roadrunner" has some serious pace (and strength).	He's super agile.
	Stop him dribbling and he'll pass it around you … or simply shoot and score. Your choice…	Nobody dribbles more (or better). His passing isn't bad either…
	Solid in defence, deadly in attack – this GOAT can do it all anywhere on the pitch.	He's fearless, unpredictable and always makes the right decision.

That's right, we're going to remind ourselves of how great these GOATs really are – with additional commentary from some legends of the game! But first we'll revisit all the key points we've made…

STATS

Saka

- He's got more goals and assists than Yamal.
- Back-to-back Player of the Season awards for club and country? Yep, that's Starboy.
- Don't underestimate his second-placed finishes – they're seriously impressive.

Yamal

- His goal contributions come at a quicker rate than Saka's!
- He's the Golden Boy who won the Kopa Trophy, too!
- He's already won a Spanish treble – and the Euros!

CONTRIBUTION

Saka

- He's taken Arsenal from "Invisibles" to challengers.
- He's one of England's most important players who's always trusted in the big moments.
- This role model is making football a kinder place.

Yamal

- He's returned Barcelona to the top of the pile in Spain – and become the Clásico King!
- He's Spain's cutting edge, their difference-maker at Euro 2024.
- This talented teen is changing Spanish attitudes towards diversity.

OUR RATINGS

	CATEGORY	SAKA	YAMAL
CHARACTER	PERSONALITY	9/10	8/10
	MINDSET	9/10	9/10
	LEADERSHIP	8/10	7/10
SKILLS	PHYSICAL SKILLS	9/10	7/10
	TECHNICAL SKILLS	8/10	9/10
	TACTICAL SKILLS	10/10	9/10
STATS	PERFORMANCE STATS	8/10	9/10
	INDIVIDUAL ACHIEVEMENTS	8/10	8/10
	TEAM TROPHIES	7/10	9/10
CONTRIBUTION	CLUB LEVEL	9/10	9/10
	COUNTRY	7/10	9/10
	THE GAME	8/10	8/10
	TOTAL RATING	100/120	101/120

OUR WINNING GOAT IS ...

YAMAL!

SAKA'S TOP MOMENTS

INTRODUCING BUKAYO

EINTRACHT FRANKFURT 0 | 3 ARSENAL

19 SEPTEMBER 2019 • EUROPA LEAGUE

Saka had only ever played seven minutes in the Premier League by the time he lined up against Eintracht Frankfurt. Yet in this Europa League tie, he announced himself, scoring one and setting up the other two. Three days later, he made his first Premier League start – and he hasn't looked back! ■

HAT-TRICK HERO

ENGLAND 7 | 0 NORTH MACEDONIA

19 JUNE 2023
EUROPEAN CHAMPIONSHIPS QUALIFYING

Saka hit his first-ever England hat-trick with a right-footed smash, a thumping half-volley from outside the area and a slotted left-footed finish in a one-v-one – all within 50 minutes! ■

THAT'S THE HALF-CENTURY!

WEST HAM 0 | 6 ARSENAL

11 FEBRUARY 2024 • PREMIER LEAGUE

Saka scored his 50th and 51st career goals for Arsenal, making it 100 goal contributions in 210 appearances – seven more than GOAT candidate Cristiano Ronaldo had after 210 appearances in his career! ■

SAKA THE SAVIOUR

ENGLAND 1 | 1 SWITZERLAND

6 JULY 2024
EUROPEAN CHAMPIONSHIPS
QUARTER-FINAL

In an unfamiliar role, at right wing back, Saka was exceptional. He equalized with a moment of individual brilliance, then buried his penalty demons from Euro 2020 to sink his spot-kick in the shootout. ■

A REAL HAMMERING

REAL MADRID 1 | 2 ARSENAL

16 APRIL 2025
CHAMPIONS LEAGUE QUARTER-FINAL

When Saka's chipped Panenka penalty was easily saved by Thibaut Courtois, Arsenal fans feared the worst. But this is Saka… He tortured Real Madrid's defence all night, scoring Arsenal's opener with a dink and making full back David Alaba's evening miserable. ■

YAMAL'S TOP MOMENTS

SPAIN, MEET YAMAL

SPAIN 3 | 3 BRAZIL

26 MARCH 2024 • INTERNATIONAL FRIENDLY

Spanish fans were licking their lips after 16-year-old Yamal's sensational performance. He set up all three goals on the night, receiving a standing ovation from the crowd at Real Madrid's Santiago Bernabéu Stadium. ■

EUROPEAN CHAMPION!

SPAIN 2 | 1 ENGLAND

14 JULY 2024 • EUROPEAN CHAMPIONSHIPS FINAL

A constant threat throughout, Yamal assisted Nico Williams for Spain's opening goal to win a major international trophy for his nation. He was later named Young Player of the Tournament. ■

MADRID MASTERCLASS

BARCELONA 3–2 REAL MADRID

26 APRIL 2025 • COPA DEL REY FINAL

To win any trophy is sweet, but to do it against your bitter rivals on the way to a domestic treble, while grabbing two assists? Yep, that'll live long in the memory. ■

YAMAL STEALS THE SHOW

BARCELONA 3–3 INTER MILAN

30 APRIL 2025
CHAMPIONS LEAGUE QUARTER-FINAL

The teenager was at his dazzling best, scoring a sensational goal, creating countless chances and dropping a dummy for Raphinha's equalizer. Yamal was at the heart of everything, taking the most shots (6), nailing the most crosses (10) and completing the most dribbles (6) of any player on the pitch. ■

TAKE THAT, FRANCE

SPAIN 5–4 FRANCE

5 JUNE 2025
UEFA NATIONS LEAGUE SEMI-FINAL

The wing wizard tortured France once again, scoring twice as Spain raced into a 5–1 lead. Though France fought back late on, the damage had already been done. ■

THE WORLD OF FOOTBALL DECIDES...

TEAM SAKA

"He's my favourite player."

THIERRY HENRY, FORMER ARSENAL AND FRANCE PLAYER

"Bukayo Saka would get in probably every team in the world."

ROY KEANE,
FOOTBALL PUNDIT AND FORMER MANCHESTER UNITED PLAYER

"He's unbelievable and one of the best players in the world right now."

GABRIEL MARTINELLI,
ARSENAL TEAMMATE

"Saka is unbelievable. There are not a lot of players like him on the planet and he is still so young. He can get better."

MIKEL ARTETA,
ARSENAL MANAGER

"If there's a better player in world football at the moment ... the only one I can think of is Lionel Messi."

TONY ADAMS,
FORMER ARSENAL PLAYER IN MARCH 2023 (A MONTH BEFORE YAMAL MADE HIS BARCELONA DEBUT!)

TEAM YAMAL

"There are players who are exceptional. And Lamine is one of them. I've always said: Lamine is a genius."

HANSI FLICK, BARCELONA MANAGER

"When you see that he has that touch, I say that he is touched by that magic wand of God, that he is different."

LUIS DE LA FUENTE, SPAIN MANAGER

"Lamine Yamal is a phenomenon born every 50 years."

SIMONE INZAGHI, INTER MILAN MANAGER

"Maradona, Messi and now Yamal."

LOTHAR MATTHÄUS, GERMANY LEGEND

"I think he's the best player in the world at the moment. Everything he does on the pitch ... just watching him play gives you that special feeling."

COLE PALMER, CHELSEA AND ENGLAND STAR

"Messi and I have already made history. Now it's Lamine Yamal's turn."

RONALDINHO, BARCELONA AND BRAZIL LEGEND

IN THE WORDS OF OTHER GOATS

"To step up the way he did. I know the mentality he's got... A fantastic night for him, and he deserved it."

HARRY KANE ON SAKA

"The stones on this guy, some player! Bukayo Saka!"

JUDE BELLINGHAM ON SAKA

"Already he's showing incredible talent. He's going to win a lot of titles, both collective and individual. He is a phenomenon."

CRISTIANO RONALDO ON YAMAL

"He is the present and, without a doubt, has a huge future."

LIONEL MESSI ON YAMAL

IN THEIR OWN WORDS

"Right now, outside of Barça, I think [Ousmane] Dembélé or Bukayo Saka are doing really well."

YAMAL IN MAY 2025

"He's top, man. Honestly, doing what he's doing at his age, what can you say, man? He's unreal... It's not normal. No one does it."

SAKA IN MAY 2025

In the words of Bukayo Saka: "I just play my game and I leave you guys to have your opinions."

Well, he's played his game(s). So that means it's time for your opinion.

We've loved arguing our points and making our cases over these pages. Even though we don't agree on many things, we can certainly say we had fun along the way. We've done our best to set you up with everything you need to know about our GOATs and their …

- Characters
- Skills
- Stats
- Contributions

So, over to you! Who's the GOAT in your opinion: Saka or Yamal? Either choice is great, and both these talents are top. But who is best?

MY WINNING GOAT IS …

____

OUT NOW!
THE FOOTBALL GOAT
WHO IS THE GREATEST OF ALL TIME?
YOU CHOOSE YOUR FAVOURITE PLAYER
MESSI V. RONALDO
MATT OLDFIELD
SETH BURKETT
THE FOOTBALL GOAT
WHO IS THE GREATEST OF ALL TIME?
YOU CHOOSE YOUR FAVOURITE PLAYER
MBAPPÉ V. HAALAND
MATT OLDFIELD
SETH BURKETT
THE FOOTBALL GOAT
WHO IS THE GREATEST OF ALL TIME?
YOU CHOOSE YOUR FAVOURITE PLAYER
PELÉ V. MARADONA
MATT OLDFIELD
SETH BURKETT
THE FOOTBALL GOAT
WHO IS THE GREATEST OF ALL TIME?
YOU CHOOSE YOUR FAVOURITE PLAYER
KANE V. BELLINGHAM
MATT OLDFIELD
SETH BURKETT
THE FOOTBALL GOAT
WHO IS THE GREATEST OF ALL TI
SAKA V. YAMAL
MATT OLDFIELD
SETH BURKETT
THE FOOTBALL GOAT
WORLD CUP EDITION!
ENGLAND V. THE WORLD
MATT OLDFIELD
SETH BURKETT
YOU CHOOSE YOUR FAVOURITE TEAM
COMING SOON!